Discover a
Richer Life

JEREMY P. TARCHER/PENGUIN

a member of Penguin Group (USA) Inc.

New York

Discover a Richer Life

Ernest Holmes

Compiled and Edited by
WILLIS KINNEAR

JEREMY P. TARCHER/PENGUIN
Published by the Penguin Group
Penguin Group (USA) Inc., 375 Hudson Street, New York, New York 10014, USA · Penguin Group
(Canada), 90 Eglinton Avenue East, Suite 700, Toronto, Ontario M4P 2Y3, Canada (a division of
Pearson Penguin Canada Inc.) · Penguin Books Ltd, 80 Strand, London WC2R 0RL, England ·
Penguin Ireland, 25 St Stephen's Green, Dublin 2, Ireland (a division of Penguin Books Ltd) ·
Penguin Group (Australia), 250 Camberwell Road, Camberwell, Victoria 3124, Australia (a division
of Pearson Australia Group Pty Ltd) · Penguin Books India Pvt Ltd, 11 Community Centre,
Panchsheel Park, New Delhi–110 017, India · Penguin Group (NZ), 67 Apollo Drive, Rosedale,
North Shore 0632, New Zealand (a division of Pearson New Zealand Ltd) · Penguin Books
(South Africa) (Pty) Ltd, 24 Sturdee Avenue, Rosebank, Johannesburg 2196, South Africa

Penguin Books Ltd, Registered Offices: 80 Strand, London WC2R 0RL, England

First Jeremy P. Tarcher/Penguin Edition 2010
Copyright © 1961 by The Church of Religious Science

Published simultaneously in Canada

Most Tarcher/Penguin books are available at special quantity discounts for bulk purchase for sales
promotions, premiums, fund-raising, and educational needs. Special books or book excerpts also can be
created to fit specific needs. For details, write Penguin Group (USA) Inc., Special Markets, 375 Hudson
Street, New York, NY 10014.

Library of Congress Cataloging-in-Publication Data

Holmes, Ernest, 1887–1960.
Discover a richer life/Ernest Holmes. —1st ed.
p.   cm.
ISBN 978-1-58542-812-0
1. Conduct of life.   2. Success.   3. Faith.   I. Title.
BJ1581.2.H618   2010   2010015348
299'.93—dc22

Printed in the United States of America
1   3   5   7   9   10   8   6   4   2

BOOK DESIGN BY NICOLE LAROCHE

While the author has made every effort to provide accurate telephone numbers and Internet addresses
at the time of publication, neither the publisher nor the author assumes any responsibility for errors, or
for changes that occur after publication. Further, the publisher does not have any control over and does
not assume any responsibility for author or third-party websites or their content.

Contents

Foreword

Ernest Holmes was one of the great spiritual leaders of our day. He always wrote and spoke with a simplicity and directness that conveyed the essence and meaning of the philosophy of Science of Mind, which he formulated and by means of which countless thousands have been able to experience a better way of life.

At the time he passed on in 1960, he left a great wealth of unpublished material, most of which will eventually appear as articles in *Science of Mind* magazine.

For over thirty years he had regular monthly features in the magazine, and this material has never been available in any other way. This volume is the first of a series that will assemble these magazine articles, bringing them together in a related manner and in a permanent form.

It is felt that each additional volume of Dr. Holmes's works will be an important contribution to his basic writings on Science of Mind.

WILLIS KINNEAR

Discover a
Richer Life

PART ONE

Foundations for Effective Living

For too long we have been dividing ourselves as well as the universe in which we live into small unrelated segments. We have been so busy doing this that we have overlooked the fact that everything is part of one stupendous whole. We have separated the spirit from the mind, and the mind from the body. We have isolated living things from that which causes them to live. The stars and the atoms we consider apart from the purposive Creativity which creates and sustains them.

There comes a time when it is necessary to try and put things back together again. We need to start to correlate and integrate the knowledge we have into a unified practical system of thought for our greater benefit in everyday living.

The ideas and wisdom expressed in the following chapters will enable you to more fully express the wonderful and complete person you are.

Philosophy

Something to Think About

Philosophy means the love of wisdom. The study of philosophy is an inquiry into the knowledge of general principles, a search after truth. Since there are many kinds of wisdom and many truths, it follows that there are many philosophies. From its broadest viewpoint the average man's philosophy is his opinion about life. The philosophy of a religious man is his opinion of the relationship between God and man. The philosophy of a businessman constitutes his speculative thought about economics. Philosophical knowledge is an attempt to establish for us a rational explanation of things as they are.

We have two general philosophical outlooks on life: one is idealistic, the other materialistic. Either one may or may not be practical. In the highest use of the term, philosophy is supposed to be ideal; hence, we have the term "idealistic philosophy" which in its extreme form means interpreting the universe purely in terms of ideas. The materialistic viewpoint of life interprets it entirely in terms of physical processes.

Until recent years the study of philosophy was held to be entirely speculative thought, a sort of Utopian dream. Those who pursued its study were considered impractical dreamers; marvelous perhaps in their mental deductions, but nevertheless pursuing a useless cause in a world of pragmatic values.

The modern philosophical outlook, however, is different. The quest after truth is now so universal that every man's mind is stimulated to inquire into the reason for things, and to study the relationships existing between the world of everyday life and action, and those higher values which we all sense. The study of philosophy is no longer looked upon as an idle speculation, a useless mental performance, entirely impractical, but is now viewed as one of the noblest pursuits to which the mind may give its attention. More books are being written on philosophy today than in any other period of history.

There is an earnest and an insistent desire on the part of ever-increasing numbers of people to discover the reason for things and the relationships existing between them, particularly in the realm of idealistic philosophy. There is an effort to discern the relationship between the Creator and creation, the invisible Cause and Its visible effect; between God, or the universal creative Spirit, and man—man being the only form of life we know of having the power to consciously and definitely sense the necessity of there being such relationships.

There is an apparent tendency in recent years among many of our scientists to turn to philosophy for a fuller explanation of their scientific findings. Today we find the study of philosophy not for those who turn from the practical values of life to daydreaming, or the courtship of mental hallucinations, but necessary to those who, having some knowledge of scientific principles and facts and some understanding of the practical values of life, still believe that there is a synthesis or a unifying Cause back of all facts.

It is from this viewpoint that we approach the study of philosophy. Like all other inquirers into truth, we have certain fundamental assumptions or beliefs which we seek to reconcile to the facts of human experience. These fundamental assumptions or beliefs are simple and few: There is an infinite creative Intelligence which creates all things by imparting of Itself to become that which is created. This original creative Cause is an indivisible unity—in Its own nature changeless and eternal—and from It proceed laws which sustain the visible universe.

It is the nature of this original Cause to continuously express, to eternally do new things; yet in doing these things It can never contradict Its own nature. The expression of this infinite Spirit in an ascending creation is what we call evolution. All things, ourselves included, are some manifestation of It; hence all things have a direct relationship to It. Since all things emerge from It and are sustained by It, and since It is all things, this relationship is direct and immediate. Our consciousness of this relationship is through an inner awareness.

This inner awareness on our part is not only our awareness of It but is also Its awareness of us. Hence our awareness of It and Its awareness of us are one and the same thing; man's consciousness of himself is God's consciousness of man. As man's consciousness expands he becomes more and more God-conscious.

Since God is infinite, the possibility of man's expansion is limitless. Therefore evolution or unfoldment is the eternal process through which Being passes into becoming. This does not make man God nor does man create God; but man at any and every level of consciousness is, at such level, a manifestation of the original Mind. As a drop of water is in the ocean, and in its essence is like the ocean, but still never is the whole ocean; so man is in God, partakes of the nature of God, in essence is One with God, but never is God. Man could never become the whole God for then he would have exhausted the possibilities of the Infinite, which by definition is an impossibility.

The progressive awakening of man to greater ideals and accomplishments, through art, science, philosophy, and religion, is the passing of Spirit through him into expression. It is the nature of this original Spirit to incarnate Itself in and as everything, to quicken all form into life, to create, sustain, promote, and expand; thus does It provide for Itself, within Itself, avenues for Self-expression and the manifestation of Its own infinite Self-knowingness.

Religion

SOMETHING TO BELIEVE

Religion means a belief in an invisible, superhuman power or powers. It is a belief in God or gods. Any system of faith, doctrine, or worship is some form of religion. So far as we know the religious sense is universal; all peoples have had some form of worship, ranging from the simplest forms of fetishism to the contemplation of pure Spirit and man's unity with It.

All religions teach the recognition of and the belief in an invisible Presence whose power and intelligence are greater than man's. The more intellectual forms of religion teach that this invisible Presence is an undivided and an indivisible unit, an omnipresent Reality.

Worship in its highest form is an attempt to identify oneself with the good, the beautiful, and the true; with love, justice, and righteousness. Religious emotion is an aspiration of the soul toward God, accompanied by a belief in an overshadowing and an indwelling Presence, and a desire to unify oneself consciously with this Presence.

Since all forms of religion have in some measure aspired toward this central goal, howsoever crude many of them may have been, each has been necessary in its day. The permanent progress of humanity is easily marked by the growth of its religious ideals.

The vitality of any religion is to be found in its affirmative and constructive beliefs. The weakness of any religion is found in its superstition, creedal pride, and dogmatic assumptions.

People are naturally religious, since through the gift of nature we all believe in some infinite Intelligence or Power. Insofar as any religion stimulates faith, this faith accomplishes definite results in the life, the character, and the outlook of the individual. Any religion which does not stimulate a positive faith in the good, the enduring, and the true, and which does not give at least some inner conviction of our identity with the Spirit, is useless; for religion is a way of life, a sentiment so pronounced that it influences every act and imagination, frees the mind and looses the spirit.

Any religion which is based on fear is negative; its evil

neutralizes its good, while too often its good fails to neutralize its evil. Our thought is torn between two opposites, hence becomes the scene of a continuous struggle; faith and failure take equal sides, doubt and fear balance trust and confidence, and man is thrown into a state of complete helplessness.

True religion should teach that there is but one ultimate Power in the universe and that this Power is good, never divided against Itself, knowing no opposites and having none, complete within Itself, yet forever unfolding.

True religion should identify man's mind with this eternal Reality and teach him that his own life is a manifestation of this universal Life; that the highest God and the innermost God is One God; that there are no opposites to good; that all beliefs in the devil, hell, evil, as things in themselves, are myths, phantasies, mistaken concepts. This the religion of the future will do—it will teach the identification of oneself with this universal Being through an inner awareness, a sense which all people have but which few people use.

The new religion will go further than this and deliberately teach a definite technique by which we will be enabled to consciously remove doubt, fear, and uncertainty from our minds and in their place create confidence and trust. For, after all, our approach to Reality is through our own minds and nowhere else. The power of spiritual conviction finds its only avenue of expression through our knowing faculties.

All revelation, inspiration, intuition, and guidance, if they are to find concrete expression, must pass through the mind. The mind is the medium through which all knowledge, all faith, all opinion, all philosophy, and all religion operate. Hence, the new religion will teach a spiritual psychology, an idealistic philosophy, and a system of metaphysics designed to consciously create in the mind a recognition and a realization that the Eternal is one with man, that the creative Intelligence of the universe is available to man, that the dynamic purposive Power which urges everything forward is latent in man, and that he can discover this Divine Presence within him. The religion of the future, then, will of necessity be a universal religion, simple and direct.

3 ·

Science

SOMETHING TO USE

S cience is an exact and systematic statement or classification of knowledge concerning some subject or group of subjects. It is the knowledge of facts, laws, and proximate causes, gained and verified by exact observations and correct thinking. The result of scientific knowledge, expressed in terms of law, gives us the ability to do something with a definite predictable result. Because we have many systems and classifications of knowledge we have many sciences, such as physics, chemistry, botany, biology, physiology, psychology. In a general way we may speak of the classified knowledge of any subject as a science.

The laws of science are universal, applicable by anyone at any time and in any place. Scientific laws, insofar as they are understood, are neutral, responding impersonally to anyone, and appear to have no self-determination. Neither could we say that the science of electricity belongs to an Edison nor the science of mathematics belongs to an Einstein, nor that any science belongs to anyone.

The increased knowledge of any science is some knowledge of universal principles which existed in their potential possibilities prior to their discovery by man. The laws of nature are her secrets unlocked by the investigating mind, which, through the intelligent understanding of man, are useful when properly applied, harmful when not rightly used.

It is now believed by many scientific minds that the material sciences can converge into one great synthesis which may be called the science of being; that a greater inclusion will tend to unify and coordinate all truths into one great system of reality, which from the religious viewpoint may be termed "the universe as a spiritual system"—One Spirit moving into many expressions. While viewing the universe as a spiritual system one need not deny the material universe; for the material universe and the laws which govern it are part of the vast system and are necessary to it.

The very word "universal" implies that the universe cannot be divided against itself. If the discovery of a new law contradicts the established facts of an older ascertained law, either the facts of the old law are false or the facts of the new law are false. The universe is so constituted that one law cannot contradict another. However, this does not mean that one law cannot transcend another. There is a law which says that anything heavier than air will fall to the ground, but by the application of the law of aerodynamics that which is heavier than air may ascend. These two laws do not contradict each other—each is a part of a whole and a unified system.

When we approach the study of the Science of Mind in its practical application we are not denying material or physical laws; we are simply introducing the use of a higher law—the law that the higher form of intelligence governs the lower, but all is part of the unified whole. The laws of psychology or metaphysics cannot neutralize or wipe out the laws of physics, nor is there any science of mind which can do away with the physiological or psychological laws of our being.

As an example let us consider the act of prayer and faith in its relation to physical healing. Many people have been healed of physical diseases through prayer and faith. The denial of this fact would be an admission of one's ignorance of such events. If the universe is an undivided system, containing as it does many laws, and containing as it must many gradations of intelligence, then it follows that when through the act of prayer and faith one is healed of some physical disability, this healing is accomplished not through the suspension of any physical law but through the recognition of the One Law which governs all. We cannot believe that God or the intelligent Life-Principle would or could violate one of His or Its laws because of any man's petition.

We cannot believe that prayer or faith changes the natural order of the universe but we do know that the act of prayer and faith does produce definite results. Hence we are compelled to admit by the very evidence of spiritual healings that something else is involved in the process.

Here is one of the apparent riddles of the universe and of our own existence. Are we living in a spiritual universe? Are we living in a mental universe? Are we living in a material universe? The extreme idealist will say we are living in a spiritual world, in a universe of pure ideas—all is mind, there is nothing else. The extreme realist will say we are living in a material universe in which mind plays no important part and in which Spirit, viewed as infinite Intelligence, plays no part. Between these two positions there appears to be a gulf which cannot be bridged. If we are living in a universe of Spirit or mind alone, then the material universe is an illusion. If we are living in a material universe alone, then mind or Spirit are fantastic concoctions of our imagination.

But how can mind be a fantastic concoction of our imagination since we are using it this moment? How can the material universe be an illusion unless mind itself is an illusion and unless all is illusion? And how can Spirit or universal Intelligence be a myth unless we, It, the material universe, and all of our mental reactions are but dreams; and to complete the argument, how can there be a dream without a dreamer?

This gulf is easily bridged if we conclude that the spiritual, mental, and physical do not contradict each other, are not divided against each other, but are one in essence; they have One Source, and function according to one great body of Law.

Let us create this new synthesis in our imagination and see what we have. If we consider that in essence the universe is one of pure Spirit, infinite Intelligence, conscious Purpose—which also acts as, and is, the source of inviolate Law by means of which It becomes universally manifested through Its energy becoming what It creates—then we find that there is room for all things. We do have a spiritual universe, we do have a mental universe of conscious thought, as well as a physical universe of tangible things; in essence they are all the same—they are but different aspects of *that* which we call God or infinite Spirit. Spirit is the all-inclusive source; thought becomes the directive factor, with manifestation being the result. But in and through all there is law which functions at every level.

Spirit is universal, Mind is universal, and so is Substance—which is pure energy becoming tangible through Law in the form provided for it by thought or idea. And whether we think of law as being spiritual, mental, or physical it makes no difference, providing we realize that the three work together in perfect unity, being but different functionings of the great Law of God. Spiritual law, mental law, and physical law are all universal and omnipresent, they all work as a unit; however, the higher form always transcends or governs the lower but never by contradicting or violating it. With this concept we can see how it is that the Spirit can govern the mind and that the right mental attitude cannot help affecting the body.

Working from such a basis we can readily see how we can by observation, experiment, and proof develop a definite technique for the practice of a true science of the mind.

4

Science of Mind

SOMETHING TO LIVE BY

On the basis of our definitions of philosophy, religion, and science, a *science* of mind becomes a definite study firmly founded on our knowledge and our highest ideals and their relationship to the great Reality, or God.

It has been said that "Thought is the activity, not the essence of the soul." The sciences of psychology and psychiatry deal largely with mental and emotional action and reaction more than with the essence. On the other hand, Science of Mind attempts to penetrate more deeply into the essence of the Spirit within man; its theoretical principle is that the real essence of man's mind and life is pure Spirit. Hence, of necessity, Science of Mind must teach *spiritual* concepts and at the same time should include in such teaching the highest and most advanced thought that can be gathered from all sources.

Science of Mind is a systematic study of the creativity of the mind of man, with its conscious and unconscious activities, and of the nature of the Spirit which has created and animates and sustains him.

Mental facts and spiritual experiences are just as real as sunsets and raindrops. One of the highest, most interesting, and illuminating pursuits to which one can give his attention is a consideration of the right relationships between the complex reactions of the mind to its external environment and its subtle reactions to Life Itself, Spirit, the great Reality, or God. We do not think of man's spirit and mind as confined within the body, but of body as being included within and sustained by the mind and spirit; and of body, mind, and spirit as being permeated or one with that higher and finer essence, which is pure Spirit—God.

A correct adjustment of one's thought in its conscious and subjective reactions to that Reality fundamental to all religions tends to produce a state of trust, of subjective harmony, of inner assurance. The physical effect of such mental adjustment is healing, for healing in its broadest and most permanent sense means harmonious action.

Thought which is continuously torn and distracted, uncertain, despondent or morbid, fearful, timid and apprehensive, produces such an inner disquiet that there is a physical correspondence resulting in irritation, inflammation, and malfunction; and, according to the testimony of our most able psychologists, psychiatrists, and doctors, may produce definite and extreme physical disabilities. This being true, they feel that a large percentage of our physical diseases would automatically disappear provided one's thoughts were properly adjusted in harmony with the environment.

Since religious emotion, culminating in a faith in God, constitutes one of our dominant motives, it follows that a spiritually oriented consciousness tends toward a physical healing; thus it is necessary, or if not necessary at least wise, to build up a true religious sentiment, high ideals, and a faith and confidence in the integrity of the universe. With our present knowledge of mental actions and reactions and with the techniques already evolved by other sciences, we have at our hands means and methods by which we may definitely neutralize wrong mental reactions and place in their stead right ideas, such as hope, trust and faith, a belief in goodness, in love, and in reason, all of which create a confidence in life. Such confidence includes a faith in one-self, and is sustained through a belief that the self is some part of the great universal Reality which sustains all through the power of Its own Self-existent Being.

A trust in God is no mere idle myth, nor can we consider

such trust a superstitious reaction to life. The greatest people who have ever lived have placed their confidence in this invisible Presence and have walked serenely through life, freed from the fears which assail and hamper the average man. We cannot doubt the reality of such experiences.

If countless numbers of people have been sustained through a calm confidence and implicit trust in Divine Intelligence, then we must accept their experiences as being valid, analyze their actions and reactions to life; and, using such affirmative facts as we may discover, build upon them the highest and most sublime hope which has ever penetrated the consciousness of man. What we must avoid, however, is the confusion which arises from a belief in final revelations, from the belief that all truth is at last discovered, or that some one person or some one system of thought has delivered the last word. There are no finalities in any science, any philosophy, or any religion. Through the continual emergence of the creative Principle any last finality proves to be but the beginning of a new creative series. This eternal spiral, finding its base in the everlasting Reality, will never cease to emerge.

Science of Mind will never be a closed book but will continue to gather spiritual truth from every source and every man's experience; and, combining them, will discover that the result is an ever-increasing revelation of the nature of the spiritual universe in which we live. Nor can we believe that any religious ideal or philosophical concept is valid if it denies the smallest fact ascertained in science. Truth will never contradict fact but will include it. Hence the religious or philosophical aspects of Science of Mind must not deny but include the findings of science through the realization that these three great branches of human knowledge, these three highways to the One Source of all things, are partners serving as guides in an endeavor to gain truth. Knowledge alone gives freedom.

Our increased awareness of spiritual truths will make each day a fresh beginning, a new approach to Reality, a spiritual adventure emerging fresh and new from the original creative Principle active within us.

PART TWO
Practical Prayer

Throughout the ages in one form or another, in one way or another, man has thought in what he considered a prayerful manner and has been able to obtain beneficial results.

Many and widely varied explanations have been advanced as to why prayer is answered, as well as to why it sometimes apparently is not answered.

One simple fact does stand out relative to any prayer: It is a certain process of thought as a result of which there are definite, specific results. Regardless of what religious, philosophical, or psychological interpretations we may desire to give to such a process of thought, prayer seems to be a universal fact effective in the lives of all men.

In view of this there must be certain common denominators, which, once known and understood, could enable any man *to so guide and direct his thinking that it could become a continuously constructive creative force in his life.*

The following pages present certain fundamental ideas, which, properly assimilated and used, will enable you to make prayer the most practical of all endeavors.

5

The Science of Prayer

IT IS DEFINITE AND CONCISE

Prayer may be considered as a spiritual mind treatment, and we use the word *spiritual* rather than Christian mind treatment, Jewish, Hindu, or some other kind of mind treatment. We use spiritual as we would use the word beauty; beauty which is the essence of the beautiful. This is why a work of art is spoken of as an object of art. Beauty itself is subjective. It projects itself into a form which is objective, but it is an objectivity of a subjective essence which is felt but not seen. We use the word spiritual in the same sense. It applies to every race, to every creed, and although we happen to be mostly Christians by background and culture, this has nothing to do with spiritual mind healing, either as a spiritual essence or as an active law or science.

We believe there is a science of right thinking which can be taught and definitely used—consciously applied with certainty of a definite result. This is also what we mean when we speak of the Science of Mind. In our way of thinking there is no such thing as a "healer" any more than there is someone who *creates* a garden, or *makes* a rose. We plant the seed; Nature creates the rose. Potentially no one has more power to heal than another. In this respect we always need to fight against superstition. It is so easy for the little truth we have to be clothed by so much superstition that finally we lose sight of its essence.

We need not be superstitious to be spiritually minded. Spiritual-mindedness is a persistent and consistent attempt to feel the Divine everywhere and in all things. It is the capacity not only to believe in but also to perceive, to feel, and to react to a unitary wholeness, an essence, an infinite personalness, a beauty, a love, and I also believe a laughter, which exists in the Universe—the Ultimate Reality. We too often get weighed down by our little virtues. Spirituality is normal, natural, spontaneous, effervescent, never studied or labored.

Spiritual mind healing, then, means exactly what it says— that the One Mind reacting on, in, through, and as the body and environment, will change a situation because we change our thinking within It. ". . . be ye transformed by the renewing of your mind. . . ." The Greeks said that man is pneuma, psyche, and soma—meaning spirit, mind, and body. The science of psychology deals with the mind; psychosomatic medicine deals with relationships between mind and body, or the mind-body unity. In addition we believe there is a unity of the Spirit and the mind, the pneuma and the psyche. Therefore, without contradicting what we may learn from other fields, we add to them and say we believe in spiritual psychosomatics. We really practice spiritual psychosomatics in spiritual mind healing because as we increase our awareness of Spirit, Its nature is expressed in our thinking. If we change our thinking, there will be a change in the body.

Mind and matter are not unrelated; in one aspect mind is intangible matter and in the other aspect it is tangible form. This is no different from Einstein saying that energy and mass are equivalent or interchangeable. He did not say that energy energizes mass, he said it may become mass. Spinoza understood this when he said mind and matter are the same thing. Therefore, in spiritual mind healing we deal with the concept that there is no difference between the essence of form and the essence in form, because the essence of form, in form, is form.

When Einstein said energy and mass are interchangeable, he did not disappear into the picture he had drawn. His identity remained that of a conscious intelligence, analyzing an energy and a mass that has intelligence but not self-awareness or consciousness. It is necessary for us to understand this, for we have an identical concept in the field of mind-body relationships—we do not deny either our body or our mind, but we do affirm Spirit, which encompasses both. We add to, but do not take from.

We understand that mind in essence and mind in form are one and the same thing. In other words, we are not trying to reach a known fact with an unknown or unknowable principle. We are not spiritualizing matter to heal disease, nor materializing spirit to perceive matter and control it. There is no such thing as a spiritual control of a material universe as though Spirit were separate from it, for such a theory involves suppositional opposites and would annihilate fundamental unity.

There is no God who is supervising a human kingdom, and there is no law in nature that contradicts another law of nature. Nature is not in conflict with itself. Nature is One system; God is One; Existence is One. Therefore, spiritual mind healing deals with the concept of disease, not as an unreality in experience, but as a wrong arrangement resulting from man's thought. And thought, rightly arranged, will automatically rearrange the condition on the basis that mind and matter are interrelated and interchangeable.

We believe in spiritual mind healing and our approach

to it is very simple. First of all, we believe that the Universe in which we live is a spiritual system governed by intelligent Law—the Law of Mind in Action.

Spiritual mind healing will not be complete until the individual is attuned to the Infinite. It will not be complete until he gets a clearance from a sense of rejection and guilt; therefore, he will have to forgive himself and others. In addition, the individual must come to realize intellectually and emotionally that there is nothing in the Universe to be afraid of. There is no fundamental evil, there is no duality. This is the essence of spiritual mind healing, and as the consciousness perceives this transcendence, it almost automatically sloughs off all other things.

There is a rhythm in the Universe, and if it were rightly understood there would be no conflict. There is a peace in the Universe, a freedom from confusion, which rightly understood would heal all troubles. There is an all-encompassing love in the Universe, which rightly understood would heal difficulties. Everything below the threshold of consciousness is subject to the level of awareness to which our consciousness has evolved. The higher form of intelligence governs the lower. Everything less than conscious intelligence is unconscious intelligence which functions either on the pattern inherent within it or injected into it by the individual mind or the race mind.

One of our greatest errors is that we sometimes think the universe was created, wound up, and is now running down, and that the Mechanic deserted it after He wound it up. God not only created the universe, but also continually expresses in and through it. Emerson said that the ancient of days is in the latest invention. He also wrote that the mind that wrote history is the mind that reads it.

It is our assumption that there is no difference between the thought and what it is going to do. What it is going to do is announced by the definiteness of the thought, but its ability to do it is not injected by the thinker. This is a very important point. For this reason I started out by saying that there are no natural "healers." In the same sense we do not say that a physicist is a natural energizer because he deals with energy. This means that the individual doesn't do the healing, but if he didn't meditate or pray, it might not be accomplished. He doesn't inject himself in the situation as a healer, but what he does is to consciously use a natural energy, intelligence, and creativity at the level of his consciousness, his recognition, and his feeling of it. In this sense the individual is a practitioner, one who uses the Law of Mind.

What, then, would be a technique of spiritual mind healing? The formation of words to conform with an idea—an idea, of course, that harms no one—and with such a conviction that they are true that nothing in your own mind, your own consciousness, rejects what you say; and then identifying what you say with the person, situation, or thing you desire to change for the good. That is all there is to it. It is simplicity itself—but it is so elusive that we look for a greater profoundness, not knowing how profound simple things are.

We of necessity believe that there is an intelligent Principle or Law in the Universe which receives the impress of our thought as we think it, and acts upon it without question, without argument, without rationality. It creates for us in our experience the content of our thought with mathematical accuracy. This is the Law of Mind. To the degree we understand our unity with Spirit, or God, and give to the Law only ideas of good, we expand our thought and free ourselves from the negative consequences of our previous limited thinking.

God is all there is; God is Perfect. There is One life, that Life is God, that Life is our life; therefore that Life is now pulsating in us. It is the everlasting Presence which is both personal and impersonal; personal as Presence and impersonal as Law. There is nothing separate from It. Now as a result of this, the logical outcome of our constructive thinking is the tangible manifestation of the good we desire, the good embodied in our prayer for the person, the affairs, or the situation we wish to help. Since the Law is everywhere and everything is in It, the desired change is initiated in the prayer itself.

The technique of application is very simple. Suppose we are praying or giving a treatment for John Doe. We might begin something like this: "This treatment is for John Doe, he lives at such and such a place. There is only God's Perfect Pattern, and that is his life now. This is the spiritual truth about him, and because it is, all which appears opposite to it is eliminated from his experience." Or we might say, "Every plant, which my heavenly Father hath not planted, shall be rooted up and cast out of his experience." These are but statements to convince the mind of the one giving the treatment; but any statement which will bring conviction is good. No two treatments can ever be alike lest we should listen to ourselves; and we must not listen to what we say but to what we really feel and think, because our speech so often affirms what we should not listen to. Let the child of simple faith within you counsel the man of experience, that the man of experience shall find out what is good and seek to follow it. The simple faith will always tell you just what to say or do.

So, there is no prescribed formula for treatment or prayer, because every time we give a treatment we must expect it to be the only time we are going to give that one. It is a new formation and must be spontaneous. The moment it becomes mechanical it seems to lose much of its power. A technique may be correct, but the fire and feeling and temperament are not always in it, and it is out of the fire of the heart that the mouth must speak. Therefore, do not wonder what words you will use. Treatment follows a Law of Intelligence and its objective manifestation corresponds to our conviction and use of that Law. Treatment is involution, manifestation is evolution; treatment is spontaneous, manifestation is mechanical.

Someone may ask, "How shall we apply this method to the treatment of affairs?" Just the same way. There is no difference between treating somebody for physical healing and treating somebody for the manifestation of needed supply. Both acts are purely mental. We reduce a condition to a mental concept and then correct what needs correcting in the mental concept. We do not deny the reality of things or affairs, but raise our own consciousness to a greater perception and acceptance of the spiritual Source of all substance and supply.

We know that thoughts have the ability of creating new experiences and conditions through the action of the One Mind. For instance, consider a person who is alone and lonely. We arrive at the conviction that there is no limitation in Spirit and no limitation in this person's life for he is One with Spirit, and new experiences are coming to him; he will meet new people, new things, new conditions. As we do this, we are setting in motion for him the Law of Mind which operates upon all things—spiritual, mental, and physical—and he will sooner or later meet whole new sets of circumstances. We must remember that out of the impulsion of our thought a creativity is set in motion which has prerogative and initiative; as the impulsion of our thought is lifted to a higher level of understanding, something new must evolve.

There is but One Creator in the Universe; we individualize It, It individualizes within us as us. There is only One Mind, we use It; One Spirit, we live by It; One Law which governs everything; One Presence which responds to everything. We are individualizations of It with the ability to initiate new causes in our experience. The Universe is not necessarily an endless and monotonous repetition of the same old thing. Every time we think, something new is being done. God is not a static God, and there is no time when creation begins; in the eternal *now,* by thought, Spirit moves upon the Law of the Universe and out of It arises a new creation.

Although it is very important to be specific in prayer or treatment, we may also initiate a new chain of causation just by affirming that something new and good is going to happen. I may send for a packet of seeds that I know nothing about and have never seen. I may never have seen the kind of flower or plant these seeds will produce. I have no mental equivalent of this particular plant in my own mind. When I subject the seeds to the creative medium of the soil they will provide me with that which I did not have an equivalent for. *My equivalent was in the ability to expect and to receive something.*

Remember this, no matter what you are treating—people or conditions—find out what is wrong, know that the opposite thought will erase it. Start as simply as that. You can do it, because nobody can think any better than you can think, and no one has any more authority about it, nobody is any better than you are. The one who is willing to abandon himself to the Genius of the Universe, to the realization of his intimate relationship to It, and who applies his thought and feeling and all that he is to this conviction, will find not a void but a solid foundation for the creation and experience of a joyous new life.

6.

The Essence of Prayer

AN EXPANDED AWARENESS

In order to help ourselves and others through prayer, I believe that we have to have a clear consciousness and a deep sense of the inward meaning of what we do. We have to have a realization that each one of us is an outlet of the Infinite because we are an inlet to It. Then I think we have to realize that there is nothing separate from God. When we use the word God we mean the Truth, Life, the Absolute, the Infinite, the Spirit; everything that means that Presence and Power and Intelligence in the universe which *is* the universe.

We are not talking about a theological God, an old man with whiskers combing his beard, soaking the Baptists and dry cleaning those who don't get immersed, or revealing Himself to the Jews and not to the Gentiles, or saving the

Adventists and ignoring the Methodists. There is no such God as the God many people believe in, and we should be very glad of that.

By the word God we mean Life, Intelligence in action, the Spirit within all nature, animating everything and animating ourselves. When we use the word God we are saluting the Divine Presence in each other and in everything—the beauty that sees and imagines and paints the glory of a sunset or the softness of an early dawn, the aroma of the rose, the enthusiasm of the child at play, the intelligence of the philosopher, the worshipful attitude of the devotee. This is all God. The moment we draw a line against some part of the eternal Presence which is in all things we shut ourselves off from It. In spiritual mind treatment, or prayer, our purpose is to become actively aware of the unrestricted wholeness of this Divine Presence.

Nothing ever happened to you or to me that need bind us if we free ourselves from the belief in it. This is why Jesus forgave people their sins. He knew that a new world is born every moment; a new spiritual time track, as it were, is created every moment. He knew that there is nothing that can bind man except ignorance of his true nature. Right now, today, any sequence of cause and effect may be intercepted and changed and everything made new in our lives. If this were not true, Jesus never would have forgiven people their sins. If this were not true, no one could be healed physically or psychologically today. Analytical psychology and psychiatry and the practice of psychosomatic medicine would be impossible, no new habits could be formed, no transcendence of ancient experience. There would be no invention in science.

That which has brought comfort to modern man, that which has brought luxury that other ages did not have, is not because the time had come when God decided to give us a gas range or an electric light or an automobile, but because man gradually accepted more of That which was there to be loosed. Out of the God that is, the world is eternally discovering a better God, and that's good.

Whatever in our experience seems to restrict, whatever appears to limit, whatever seems to be the cause of our disturbances must be negated. Now that means that we turn from all our beliefs of bondage, whatever they may be. It doesn't matter who or how many people have believed in them, God the Absolute, God the limitless Infinite, God the eternal Love and Givingness, is right where we are, in fullness. Our own past must not be held against us else we create a new bondage out of the old image.

As we turn within to that Divine Presence, we know that all the ages of the past, all the experiences we have ever had, do not matter today. Here and now we stand forth free from the burden of the past. If there has been what the world calls sin, we are forgiven. If there has been a sense of rejection, we now know that we are included in the Divine Love and Wisdom. If there has been a sense of separation, we now reunite our imagination and will with That from which we have never been separated, nor could have been. There is One Life, and we are that Life. "I am that which Thou art, Thou art that which I am"—eternal and perfect, forever blessed. Within each one of us, circulating and flowing with the rhythm of the heartbeat of the Universe is but the one heart. There is but one circulation, unimpeded by anything we have done, and that whole system of circulation is the harmony and the joy of the flow and the return circuit of Divine Intelligence and Wisdom.

We are guided and governed and sustained by infinite Mind which knows what to do within us, how to do it, and does it. There is One Mind, that Mind is God, that Mind is in what we are doing. The eternal process of that Mind, forever manifesting Its limitless imagination and activity, is at the point of our own intelligence, thinking in what we are thinking, creating in what we are doing, and being what we are. There is nothing else. And we shall not be bound even by our own mistakes.

We let no doubt or fear or thought of limitation restrict the flow of That which is omnipotent and present and forever blessed. We are animated by the Essence of vitality and energy, we are stimulated by the enthusiastic imagination and will of That which creates everything in the universe, and we abide in the stillness and tranquillity and calm of the infinite Peace which knows no confusion or fear, the eternal Life which needs no resurrection.

Transcendent, triumphant, new and perfect, springing perennially from the heart of the Universe is our own heart and mind and will and imagination. All creation is a proclamation of the Creator. All that is beautiful is the atmosphere of that eternal Beauty and flows in harmony and symmetry through everything and makes one grand music of the spheres—the only Presence in everything, the God eternal. We identify ourselves with this living Presence.

7

Using the Law of Mind

A Response to Every Thought

There is a Law of Mind in action, Intelligence taking form through Law; and Its action in our experience can only be a result of motivation by our thought.

This probably confuses many, for most people are a little bit superstitious when they come to think of things spiritual, not realizing that everything in the universe has to be governed by law and order; that there would have to be laws of Mind or Spirit, just as there are physical laws. This is why Jesus said it is done unto us *as* we believe. There is *something* that does it, but only *as we believe;* therefore it responds to us by corresponding with our acceptance of it. Now at first this seems a little difficult and hard to accept and it looks as though we couldn't understand it; but what do we really understand? We do not understand how acorns become oak trees, we do not understand anything other than the *way* nature works. The *why* and *how*, science, philosophy, and religion know nothing about, and these are the only avenues of knowledge we have. If, then, we had the same faith in spiritual law that we do and must have in everything we deal with in nature we would have perfect faith, because we wouldn't doubt and seeming miracles would happen every day.

I would like to establish why I believe that we can use the Law of Mind and use It independently of our present circumstances, The principle upon which Its use is based involves two very simple theories: The universe in which we live is a thing of Intelligence, and of Presence. Sir James Jeans, the great astronomer, said that we could think of God as "an infinite thinker thinking mathematically"; by which he meant there is Person—the thoughts of God and the Law of God. Sir Arthur Eddington, another famous astronomer, said that all physical laws appear as though "they were intelligence acting as law." Now this is exactly what I believe: We as persons live in a Divine Presence as spirit and in a universal Law as action; and we should receive inspiration from the one and give direction to the other. We are surrounded by an Intelligence which receives the impress of our thought and acts upon it. It also could only be the ultimate Creative

Agency in the universe which responds to us, much as the image of an object is reflected to us from a mirror. It is done unto us *as* we believe, and we are forgiven our debts *as* we forgive our debtors.

To this we must add one other thought: The subjective state of our thought constitutes ninety percent of our total thought content, maybe ninety-nine percent. All these unconscious thoughts and thought patterns—motivations, conflicts, repressions, whatever you want to call them—are beneath our conscious threshold, but they also help to constitute our entire thought! If we could come to understand that the Law of Mind responds to our entire content of thought, we should see that habitual thought patterns, even though unconscious, would be silently attracting or repelling whether we knew it or not. It is just as though all of our pockets were full of different kinds of seeds and as we walked around they kept falling out into the ground; whether we knew it or not, they would produce growth. We would then look about and say, "I did not sow these seeds." We have done it unknowingly, but ignorance of the Law excuses no one from Its operation.

We must realize that what all the world has believed influences our thought. This is the theory that Carl Jung, the great psychiatrist, developed. In addition to his psychological and medical outlook he also has sound spiritual and metaphysical concepts and he sees the universe as one system. He refers to the sum total of the world thought as the collective unconscious, and what everybody believes in some way operates through everyone else.

In analytical psychology it is recognized that most of our repressed thoughts do not come back into the conscious mind. If so, we should not be surprised that all of us are carrying around thoughts that in some way deny the supremacy of Good. In my estimation, if we could get the majority of the people in the world today to believing and affirming that there need never be another war, there never would be another one. It is the only thing that can stop war, everything else tends to bring it on. This is the only thing that can stop war, whether it is called a prayer of faith or science of mind—it doesn't matter. However, world peace can only happen when the sum total of the people's belief adds up to the fact that it is going to come about.

We do know that one kind of thought can neutralize another. This is very important. Otherwise, if we are full of negative thoughts and they are attracting negative conditions, and if we could not change them then we would be caught in a trap. Fortunately, this is not the case. One kind of thought will replace another. This has already been determined in at least two laboratory projects—at Duke University and University of Redlands. The results indicate that affirmative prayer neutralizes previous negative prayer. These scientific demonstrations indicate that no matter how much anybody failed, if he could affirm success he could neutralize the failure. Isn't it a rather remarkable thing that this finding came from psychological laboratories rather than theological seminaries? It appears to be a paradox, similar to the situation Jesus encountered. He had to find his followers from doctors, lawyers, fishermen, and tax collectors. Why? The priests could not free themselves from old static thought patterns.

I believe we are all somewhat that way. So we find today that some great spiritual truths are being demonstrated in scientific endeavors, and we should be glad of it. I am always glad when new findings in physics, psychology, or medicine have a significance or meaning which exactly parallels what you and I believe and helps to prove it. This, modern science is continually doing. It is now demonstrated—and is no different from what Jesus implied—that affirmative prayer outweighs negative prayer and we may take that to mean that conscious affirmation will neutralize an unconscious negation.

What does this mean?

Suppose somebody has been filled with fear all his life. Fear is sort of a vague thing, often one does not know what he is afraid of, but he is afraid. But if we know that a thought of faith will neutralize a thought of fear in ourselves, or somebody else, and that a continuous conscious affirmative attitude will neutralize a negative one; if we come to know that one kind of thought will neutralize another, wipe it out, then we can set about to change our thinking and our world of experience.

As we entertain new and desirable thoughts in consciousness they in turn become part of the content of the subconscious and gradually the entire content of our thought can be swung over from what perhaps has been negative to what is positive. And as we do this the Law of Mind responds accordingly, and that which is created as our experience comes to reflect the new content of our thought and so we start to live a new life. We give thanks that God, who created all things, has given us the ways and the means to more fully express His Life which is within us, and to discover and experience joy and happiness in all that we are and do.

8.

The Way Prayer Works

As You Believe It Works

What do we mean when we say there is a principle of scientific prayer? What enables a prayer to be answered is the affirmative acceptance that it is already answered! This is not a bit different from what Jesus taught. We are gradually outgrowing our stupidity and gradually catching up to the magnificence and brilliance of the greatest mind that ever graced this planet, that shot like a meteor across it in a few brief years and left behind a trail which all the world seeks to follow.

He said: "I and my Father are one." ". . . What things soever ye desire when ye pray, believe that ye receive them, and ye shall have them." How could it be otherwise? If the universe is a spiritual system governed by Intelligence, and the

Law of Mind in action, then it follows that you and I cannot get outside of the universe in which we live. We must obey its Law through understanding It, or in ignorance disobey It. This is why Emerson said: "There is no sin but ignorance, and no salvation but enlightenment." And he was right.

The prayer that accepts its answer complies with the Law of the universe. Why? Because that is the way the universe is organized, and that is its nature. It could not be otherwise and remain self-existent. We are dealing with a natural, spontaneous Power that all we can say of It is, "It is." All we can say of Its operation is, "This is the way It works." All we can do with It is, "Cooperate with Its Law and then Its Power and Energy are available." There is an ancient saying: Nature obeys us as we first obey it. Every scientist knows he must adhere to the law governing the principle he utilizes or nothing will happen.

It so happens and it is so demonstrated that this principle of prayer works! Remember, it was a little child that Jesus pressed into service to multiply the loaves and fishes. Of the great and wise that were there, all said it could not be done. But Jesus knew the Principle with which he worked, his God, and in all this vast throng he had to turn to a little boy to help him, one who did not know it could not be done.

To know that prayer works definitely and specifically is to realize that its creative Power is within us. The Power we do not create. If you and I had to create energy where would we find the energy with which to create energy? "'Tis Thou God who giveth, 'tis I who receive." Every scientist knows that he is a beneficiary of the Divine fact, and that is the way it is. We must *accept*, and not because God would be angry with us if we do not.

To believe is the prime requisite. It is done unto you as you believe is the simple explanation of effective prayer as stated by Jesus. He spoke both from a consciousness of God within him and as a Son of God. He also realized "The Son can do nothing of himself, but what he seeth the Father do: for what things soever he doeth, these also doeth the Son likewise . . . that the Father may be glorified in the Son."

A centurion came to Jesus one day and said, in effect, "I also am a man in authority. I say to one do this, and to another do that, and they do it. I understand the meaning of authority"—in our terminology he meant that he had the mental equivalent of authority—"You need speak the word only, and my servant shall be healed." Jesus turned around, amazed. He was filled with admiration and exclaimed, ". . . I have not found so great faith, no, not in Israel . . . Go thy way; and as thou hast believed, so be it done unto thee. And his servant was healed in the selfsame hour." This was done through natural Energy, Power, creative Intelligence, life-giving Force—call it what you will.

That is the principle of the answer to prayer, delivered two thousand years ago. We are gradually catching up. But up until recently, with very few exceptions, the people who discovered it thought God had patted them on the back and said, "Here is the whole works, anyone who denies your authority, blasphemes." This is nonsense. Is it not strange how difficult it is for the human mind to finally conceive of itself as free, no longer bound, free under the great Law of all life? Every man must finally come to be his own revealer of truth. No man shall enter the sacred and secret precinct of the Most High for you or for me, but each in the silence of his own soul, in the integrity of his own spirit, and the volition of his own choice shall walk into the Holy of Holies and discover God within himself.

This is the secret and simplicity of prayer. The profoundness of simplicity is one of the things that is most often overlooked in philosophy. We have to come right back to simple fact and say the nature of Reality is such, the nature of God is such, the nature of the Law of Being is such, my nature is such, that in some way, whether I understand it or not, I am so much a part of Reality that my thoughts, while they are not creative of themselves, are creative because they deal with *creativity*. And that is the way it is.

Therefore, those thoughts which are affirmative, those thoughts which embody and accept, are like the nature of the creative thinking of God which cannot conceive anything other than Himself. In such degree, then, as I assume this affirmative attitude toward the Universe and embody the meaning of goodness and truth and beauty, so shall they "follow me all the days of my life: and I will dwell in the house of the Lord for ever." How simple! But I can take each of these simple statements and surround it with words that make it as difficult to understand as Plato or Aristotle. Jesus said that it was done unto us as we believe and he didn't try to explain it because he knew it couldn't be explained.

The nature of God, the nature of the Universe and Its Law, our nature and our relationship to this Universe just are, and are universal. And science has learned long since when a principle is deduced and demonstrated to exist there is no argument as whether to label it Methodist or Catholic or anything else. Who cares? It works. And you can benefit from it just as much as anyone else can.

A youngster was drawing a picture and someone asked him what he was doing. He replied, "I am making a picture of God." The wise man said, "But you don't know what God looks like, do you?" The youngster answered, "I don't now, but I will know in a few minutes." He didn't have a guilt complex, so his picture of God was going to be a good one.

In a certain sense, out of the Divine possibility of everything, you and I create each day a better concept of God, drawing closer to the Divine Presence we believe in. We are to believe, to accept, to affirm, and to embody It, not deny It. But there are certain implications. We shall never know that God is Love unless we love. We shall never know that God is Peace, while we are disturbed. Otherwise, it is all a theory. That is the way it works and all the beseeching on earth will not change one bit of it. There is no way to contradict the Law of the Universe. Peace begets peace; love begets love; tranquillity gives birth to tranquillity; opulence, supply, and everything that is the answer to human need is not in a thin dime, but in a concept of abundance that flows evermore.

Because the Universe is one of Law and Order there is an exact, mathematical, mechanical, irresistible, irrevocable, and immutable reaction to our thoughts. It is done unto you and unto me and to all *exactly* as we believe.

Individually and collectively let those of us who espouse the cause of a new spiritual freedom enjoy to drink from the waters of increased knowledge, and in gladness distribute the good we have to the four winds of heaven. Let us keep persistently in our minds that it is our desire, individually and collectively, that everything we touch shall be healed, every person made glad, every situation properly revitalized.

PART THREE

Discover Your Place in Life

All too many people go through life without ever feeling that they are in their right place, achieving a satisfactory degree of success, or enjoying good health or companionship. Yet at the same time they see all about them others who do seem to have an adequate share of such things. Does the Universe play favorites?

It may be said that the Universe appears to favor some more than others, but only because an individual first comes to recognize the nature of the Universe and avail himself of Its potentialities.

To what extent does an individual consider himself part of or outside the scheme of things? Does he feel that he is an isolated bit of life waging a futile battle against insurmountable odds in a hostile world? or does he consider himself to be the continual beneficiary of all the good that is available?

Wherever you find yourself today, or wherever you hope to

*be tomorrow, depends upon what you consider to be your re-
lationship to that which creates and sustains all things. The
discovery of a new and better place in life demands a greater
concept of Life and the definite application of that concept in
a practical way.*

*The views expressed in the next chapters may enable you
to expand your thinking so that you can permit yourself to
accept your heart's desires.*

9

Start to Live a New Life

It Is Available Now

Let us never forget that everyone is a center in the Consciousness of God, and no one is more important than another. Every man is on the pathway of an eternal evolution.

We must never deviate from the two fundamental propositions of the ages: The Universe is impelled by Love and propelled by Law. These are the two great realities and their action and reaction constitute the mystery of the Universe in which we live, declaring Its Self-Existence, and filling the mind with wonder and with awe.

When Jesus asked his disciples who the multitudes thought he was, they replied that some thought he was a prophet come to earth again, and some thought that he was the long-awaited Messiah. Jesus then turned to the impetuous Peter and asked: "But whom say ye that I am?" Peter, with one of those quick flashes of intuition of his, said: "Thou art the Christ, the Son of the living God." And Jesus replied that flesh and blood had not revealed this to Peter, but the God indwelling had lifted the veil of sleep that hangs so heavy over the eyes of man and Peter had seen what Jesus came to proclaim: the truth about man himself.

We must penetrate more deeply into the nature, meaning, and wonder of the living Christ, not as a historic Jesus, but as that which lives and moves and breathes today in each one of us. If God is omnipresent, God is both overdwelling and indwelling; the highest God and the innermost God are the same God. No man hath seen God, only the Son hath revealed Him, which Son all mankind is. Not by virtue of any good thing that we have ever done are we that Son; nor by any evil that we have ever done shall we lose one iota of that Divinity. The dismal story of sin and salvation does not belong to the new order of thought which is enlightening the world. "The kingdom of God is at hand."

I have never met and know that I shall never meet one single individual who, having gotten a clearance for himself, has ever denied it to anyone else. I know in such degree as you and I condemn anyone, we are not sure of ourselves.

Harmony knows nothing of discord; love has never heard of hate. God is not acquainted with the devil. God is transcendent, and immanent, and omnipresent. It is only as we translate the commonplace into the terms of the transcendence that we shall recognize and realize the immanence; it is only when we elevate the commonplace to the mountaintops that we shall understand and enter into the transcendence. For they are one and the same, equal and identical, even as the Divine Spirit is equally omnipresent throughout the vast Cosmos—not moving, but causing everything within It to move.

Every day is a fresh beginning, every day is the world made new. And when we discover that split second beyond time that Jesus and all the great, good, and wise have told us about—that moment in the eternal present when we are no longer conditioned by the past and when anticipation of the future does not condition the present—we shall be free.

All creation, in my estimation, exists as the expression of God, a Self-Expression of the Infinite; the articulation of That which needs instrumentality for Its own identity. Therefore only as you and I, with wonder, reverence, and enthusiasm, identify ourselves with the living Spirit can we hope that the living Spirit, through this instrumentality, shall shape the course of our existence and sing the song of eternity in us. Identified with Divine Givingness, the human surrendering itself to intuition shall speak the language of eternity.

This is the greatest revelation we can have. Find one man or woman or child who has become acquainted with the Divine Presence and you will learn more from him than from all the books you can ever read. There is an integrity beyond ours, there is an imagination beyond ours, there is a feeling deeper than ours, and yet we are akin to it. Who listens closely to his own spirit shall hear a song no other person can sing. Who listens to the harmony of his own being, though he be in the desert or on the mountaintop alone, shall compose a symphony which no instrument can be attuned to, for it can be played only on the harp strings of his own heart, his own mind.

There is hidden within the mind of man a Divinity; there is incarnated in you and in me that which is an incarnation of God. This Divine Sonship is not a projection of that which is unlike our nature, it is not a projection of the Divine into the human. God cannot project Himself outside Himself; God can only express Himself within Himself. There is and can be no such thing as a distinct or separate individual that would be separate from the Universe.

An "individual" means something separate from something else. Man is not an individual *in* God, for this would presuppose isolation and separation and disunion. Man is an individualization *of* God. "He that hath seen me hath seen the Father." Unity permits of no division; the altar of God will not accept the gift made in the sense of isolation, of fear, or appeasement. It is only the pure in heart, the childlike in mind, and the meek who can see Him. There is no arrogance in spirituality, for intellectual arrogance is spiritual blindness. The stupidity, the ignorance, the futility, and the littleness of the intellect is a crime against the Spirit, a denial of that sublime Thing within us which waits to take flight to more of the complete, more of the perfect.

What was it that Jesus proclaimed? "I am the way, the truth, and the life: no man cometh unto the Father, but by me." He was not talking about Jesus, he was talking about *you*. Jesus gave us back to ourselves. How are you ever going to consciously reach God other than through your own nature? There are no prophets other than the wise. There is no God beyond Truth, and no revelation higher than the realization of the Divinity within us. That which the ages have failed to reveal, you and I must reveal; each to himself in the secret chamber of his own heart, the secret place of the Most High, where only and alone does one abide under the shadow of the Almighty. This aloneness is not a loneliness; it is the one all-inclusive, all-penetrating unity of everything that is.

This was the claim Jesus made upon the Universe, and we must do the same; identify ourselves with the same Presence, the same Person, and the same Principle. The mind and the spirit cannot help but generate love. Since we are one with all life, we wish to express the most life that we can— your life is my life, my life is your life. I cannot leave you out and understand myself. I am incomplete. I am lame and blind and halt without inclusion. Our littleness, the narrow vision of our spiritual perspective causes the horizon of God's boundless skies to press so close to us that we are suffocated by that which alone can give life. We must reverse the process.

The Eternal, the Everlasting, the Infinite knows nothing about our little ways, our petty thoughts, our little divisions and subdivisions that stifle the mind, the intellect, and the imagination. We have tried to contain the Infinite in a small measure that will not hold It. We have tried to reduce the Eternal to the level of the temporal, and the temporal cannot contain It. In our anguish we have beseeched the living God to save us from limitation, but it is we alone who can free ourselves.

Some day when we come to the great Reality in adoration, having surrendered our littleness, our hopes, our fears, our longings, our heavens, our hells; when we come naked and clean and unafraid, then shall our horizon be extended and the night shall cease. Then shall our valleys be elevated to the mountaintops and God Himself shall go forth anew into creation through you and through me, lighting our path to the indwelling city of God at the center of our own being.

The Universe Is for You

START TO USE IT

There is an old Chinese proverb that says: "Tomorrow's plants are in today's seeds." And our Bible speaks of the time when the plant was in the seed before the seed was in the ground. In other words, they are both saying that everything we see comes from the invisible through some silent process of nature that we know nothing about. Think of the process of the building of the human body; through food and liquids, and by some inner chemistry which is beyond the ingenuity of man, our hair, our feet, our fingers, our internal organs, the blood and bones and tissues are created from some design and by some pattern which no man has ever seen.

No artist ever sees beauty, he feels it; it is an invisible

thing. No psychologist has ever seen the mind. All the biologists in the world have no more idea how we can live than a child has. They watch the process, they see the performance, they know what happens, but that invisible thing, the unknown *guest*, they know nothing about. We know very well that within us some invisible Presence, some unknown *guest* animates and sustains; and the moment It severs Itself from the body, the body begins to disintegrate. It is certain that the integrating factor has left.

Somebody said: "Lord, for tomorrow and its needs I do not pray. But make me to do Thy will, dear Lord, just for today." Let's couple that idea with the Chinese proverb that tomorrow's plants are in the seeds of today, and let's couple it with something that Jesus said, because he was the wisest of the wise: "What things soever ye desire, when ye pray, believe that ye receive them, and ye shall have them." Then he said something else equally as interesting: "Judge not according to the appearance, but judge righteous judgment."

For instance, if we were planting an acorn we would not judge according to appearances. We would merely make a little hole in the soil and put in it a small seed no larger than a marble. We would not see an oak tree but it is there in the acorn, in the action of the law that is going to produce it. And even if there never had been an oak tree before, it would still grow. It is the same with everything in life—all of its vital processes are invisible. We do not see them; we do not hear them; in only a very indefinite sense do we really feel them, but we do see evidence of them everywhere about us. In the springtime we see that the seed is bursting forth to produce a plant and the plant produces a blossom and the blossom another seed. And so we find that all of these silent creative processes are going on. That which created the Universe is creating us now. And when Jesus said when you pray believe that you have he was announcing the Law of Cause and Effect that is valid in the world of mind and spirit. For the Universe is one system containing one body of Law, which may be interpreted in terms of what is called spiritual law, mental law, or physical law.

We can choose to plant a seed in the ground and some natural process will operate upon it to produce a plant that is like the pattern in the seed, independently of us. Does this not really explain how it is that faith operates? Everybody is familiar with the idea that faith can produce a result, but how few people ever stop to analyze why, or how, or just what is faith. It is true that faith is an attitude we have toward that Power greater than we are, but it is also a mental attitude that we sustain in our own mind about the operation, action, or reaction of that Power toward us. In other words, faith, if we will strip it of all things but what it really is and view it with complete objectivity and reality, is a way of thinking or believing which admits of no doubt, which accepts a proposition whether seen or not, judges not according to appearances, believes that the future flows out of the present, believes that the future is changed when the present is changed, that the seeds of today produce the plants of tomorrow, and that the thoughts of today produce the events of the future.

I think we should come to believe that the Universe is good. No matter what happens, disregarding everything we may see, the Universe Itself has to be good or you and I wouldn't be here. It has to be constructive or It would destroy Itself. We may be certain that whoever complies with the laws of nature will find the laws of nature complying with him. But somehow or other we haven't quite thought that spiritual and mental laws are just as real as physical ones. And yet today in psychosomatic medicine, in psychiatry and psychology and allied branches of the science of mind, we are definitely discovering how the silent processes of our own emotional reactions and our patterns of thinking are the seeds of what tomorrow will be; the fruitage will be in our physical bodies, in our relationships, and in our environment.

We must know that the Universe is for us and not against

us. Therefore it seems to me we should have a quiet sense of childlike trust and faith. Too many people are so afraid of God and the future, and have become so wrapped up with some dismal philosophy, that they feel something bad is going to happen to them. It doesn't need to. You and I do not have to assume the burdens and the obligations and the responsibilities of the Universe. It carries us; we do not carry It. But we certainly have to comply with Its laws. They are creative; they are good. This is why Jesus said that if you want to be forgiven you have to forgive. And this is only the natural Law of Cause and Effect. If we constructively use It then we have a good reason to expect that something good will happen. If we wish to change our thinking we can change our lives.

If our experiences are the result of our thoughts, then the future, if it is going to be given birth to in the present, will be largely the lengthened shadow of the content of our minds, of our feelings of faith or fear. It is no wonder that the future so seldom becomes better than the past, and often worse as pessimism takes the place of optimism. We have to learn to speak an affirmative language. An affirmative language is creative of good. We must learn to say, "Tomorrow is going to be a good day." Someone may laugh and say, "But look at what happened yesterday?" But did you know that the first boat which crossed the Atlantic driven by steam carried in her cabin a scientific treatise of that day explaining exactly why it was that no boat could be propelled by steam?

It is very characteristic of the human mind to consider that everything that is good, everything that is optimistic, either belongs to some future state or that it is withheld from us, or that we are not good enough to receive it, or that there is some reason why it should not come into our experience. And yet, those whose faith is based on the thought and the philosophy and the experience of one whom we consider to have been the greatest spiritual genius who ever lived, are not reading his words very carefully, for he said: ". . . as thou hast believed, so be it done unto thee."

I suggest that we forget all of the past, and not wonder too much if faith works, but accept; that we start to remake and remodel our own thinking. Here is an interesting thing that happens when we do this. Out of the past comes a sort of a repetition, like a monotonous song being sung: "It can't be this way. It is too good to be true. I don't know how to do it. I am not good enough to do it. Who said it's true?" You know all the arguments. Where do they come from? It is a well-recognized fact in psychology and psychiatry today that all the morbid and unhappy thought patterns which we have ever had repeat themselves, as they say, with monotonous regularity and that they actually resist any change of thought. Well, let's recognize this as a law of our psychological nature and not be disturbed by it; but, by recognizing it, we then know what we are dealing with; and knowing what we are dealing with, we shall know how to deal with it.

It isn't always easy, but we can determine to do it; and I think there is one first step we need to take and that is to resolve to make our emotions and our thoughts a little more optimistic, a little more affirmative, a little more enjoyable. What difference does it make if somebody thinks, "Well, it's an illusion. It's Pollyannish"? Did you ever stop to think that no one is ever going to live for you but yourself? No one can be unhappy for you but yourself; no one can be happy for you but yourself. And it doesn't make a particle of difference what all the world thinks, if you and I know something constructive about ourselves. We need not fall into the error of believing what everybody around us believes, or in what the world has always experienced.

As we press forward into the future certainly we should carry with us everything out of the experience of the past which was of the nature of love, truth, beauty, faith, reason, and goodness, and everything that has optimism; and certainly we should tend to discard everything that is discouraging. We should create a greater sense of flexibility, of love, a greater sense of tolerance, a deeper feeling for others, for the universe. Every psychologist tells us there are four adjustments: with the self, with the family, with society; then with the universe. How right they are when they say that first I must change my own thinking; then I must make an adjustment to those immediately around me because they are the ones with whom I am most intimately associated; next, it must be with society itself; and last of all, with the universe in which I live. But the interesting thing is the first adjustment with the self; it is the only real adjustment we ever have to make for when this is properly done we are automatically adjusted to all other things.

The seeds of today are the fruits of tomorrow, and we shall be happy indeed on the morrow if the seeds we plant today are seeds of love, and faith, and good will; for "There is no unbelief; Whoever plants a seed beneath the sod and waits to see it push away the clod, He trusts in God."

Stars, Atoms, and Men

RECOGNIZE YOUR IMPORTANCE

It was one of the Greek philosophers who first said everything was made of atoms. Now we say atoms are made of positive and negative charges of electricity—pure energy. No one has seen them, but out of that which we do not see emerges that which we do see. The biggest thing in the universe is just made up out of the littlest things. You put a lot of the littlest things together and the only difference is in the outline or form and not in the substance or the law through which they are created. As far as God, or the Creative Genius of the universe, is concerned there is no big and no little, no hard and no easy, no good and no bad.

You and I right now are living in a universe where the only difference between a star and an atom is in the concept

of the man who perceives them. This is the prime relationship. So far as creation is concerned, mankind alone knows
a star and an atom; and wouldn't it be strange if we came to
see that we alone know heaven and hell, abundance and impoverishment, health and sickness, good and bad? That is
why the Bhagavad-Gita says that the self must raise the self
by the self. I think Shakespeare understood it also when
he said: "To thine own self be true, and it must follow as
the night the day thou canst not then be false to any man."
Shakespeare did not say "thou wilt not"; he said "thou *canst*
not then be false to any man." And Browning, speaking of
the soul, said: "What entered into thee was, is, and shall be."
In other words, these great thinkers have tried to tell us that
we are not separate from God. There is already Something
within us which is transcendent and triumphant, not only
eternal in the duration of time, but omnipresent in the time
in which we live. They did not say, "Man, you are put on
earth to save your soul"—not the great ones, only the lesser
ones said this. They were the ones who had psychological
complexes and psychological frustrations that produced a
sense of guilt, which they projected into other people and
the universe in order to get a release from their own conflict
and anguish.

The great ones were the ones who saw and knew. The
interesting thing is that modern science is substantiating

their declarations. Modern physics is almost metaphysics. One of the leading authorities in science said the new interpretation of physics makes it look as though everything in the universe is like a shadow cast by an invisible substance. The Bible says "faith is the substance of" *that thing* and will produce its own evidence. And so atoms, the infinitesimal— the little things we don't see—are there all right; but the meaning they have to us as individuals is the meaning we give to them! What is our own vision? What is our own thought?

These men have said that the Universe is in equal balance, so that to each one of us, because each one of us is an incarnation of God, the Universe reveals as much of Itself as we can come to see. This is one of the greatest things in our philosophy. Lots of people say to me, "I don't understand"; and I say, "Wait until you do; keep at it until you do." It is not a spiritual grab bag, but it is nice if you have a stomach-ache to get over it; nice if you have a big headache to get it removed; nice if you need money to get it. I believe in all these things. But how much better it would be if we saw behind it all to the Source. I would rather know that I shall always be happy, which I generally am; that I shall always live, which I know I shall somewhere. I would rather know and be certain that I am in league with That which is both big and little and doesn't know the difference, each is merely an expression of Itself; that the laugh of a child is equal to the building of a kingdom; and the crooning of a mother's love over the babe at her breast is no different from the eternal Heart of the Universe surrendering everything It has in the affection of Its own Self-givingness that It may more completely come into the expression of Its own Love.

All the art and science of the human mind cannot deter, or vary temporarily, its own evolution. Let us not be afraid, let's dare to face things as they are, and not shun the Reality which some day, sooner or later, we will have to face, for we will never be saved from the stupidity of our own ignorance until we do. We are slaves, bound by the chains of our own littleness. We are infinite beings restricting ourselves to the finite sense of things. This the great have known.

Ignorance traps us mathematically and we have to free ourselves from the thralldom of the thought that something is big or little, infinite or finite; until at last we see there is One God over all, in all, and through all. And shall He not clothe Himself in garments of light in what we call big, and seem to be obscure in what we call little? Is there more life in an elephant than there is in a flea because the elephant is bigger? I don't think so at all. And we have to come to realize the atoms and the stars—the infinitesimal, the little—and that which seems to be of great magnitude—the big—are but different expressions of the One that is neither little nor big, and that each one of us must exist here for the expression of the eternal Creator—Mind, God.

What else could we be here for? It is no different from Jesus saying "I am come that they might have life, and that they might have it more abundantly"; or Tennyson saying in *In Memoriam*: "Strong son of God, immortal love, Whom we, that have not seen thy face, By faith, and faith alone, embrace, Believing where we cannot prove . . . One God, one law, one element, And one far-off divine event, To which the whole creation moves." This is the perception of a poet who feels, by intuition, the irresistible Reality that clothes Itself in every form, sings with every song, writes every poem, creates every invention, and enjoys Itself through our acts. I believe this.

Our ignorance creates our limitation of the Infinite's flow in us. Why else would Jesus say it is done unto us as we believe? We are the measurer-outer. Psychosomatic medicine is proving in its field that the very power that makes us sick can heal us. But we view ourselves so finitely, so isolated, so separated, we do not seem to know that the Power of the Infinite flows through that which is big and little, that the creative imagination of the Infinite is over all, in all, and through all, and that energy and mass, or the invisible and visible, have equality and are interchangeable.

In one sense the stars are not big, the atoms are not little, because fundamentally they can be resolved into the same primary essence or energy. One is made up of a lot of the others. Who can say there is any great and small to the Soul that maketh all? It is absolutely impossible. Neither can we say one man has or possesses more power than another. One man may use more power than another, but we all use the same Power. One man does not have greater joy than another; he may experience greater joy. Every man has all the joy there is. If we could see this we could see that the relationship between the finite and the Infinite is one of identity. Each of us is one with It and as much of It as he incorporates in his own consciousness shall flow through him as power, as love, as joy.

Then, if we find ourselves in bondage, and through ignorance we have created for ourselves a pattern of futility and a future of condemnation, we have to know that there is no condemnation, no judgment, no restriction imposed upon us by the eternal Presence. The Eternal is not static in the temporal; the Infinite is not bound by the finite, nor is God restricted by man. The slightest act or thought of ours, like the atom, can be multiplied into an aggregate of great magnitude. The bigness or littleness, the goodness or badness of our experience is equal to the invisible pattern we have created for it through the process of our own thought. They are the same thing.

12

Unlimited Living

Free Your Thinking

The universe is abundant, unlimited in every respect; if it were not unlimited it would have depleted itself long, long ago. Life would have exhausted itself, law would have ceased to function, love would have lost its power to harmonize and to heal, and thought and consciousness would have retreated to instinctive reaction. Instead, what do we find? The fish in the ocean lay so many eggs that if they all hatched the waters would overflow all the lowlands. The stars in the heavens are beyond counting. The grains of sand on the beaches are innumerable. The leaves on the trees continue to multiply. Nature is lavish, abundant, extravagant.

Why? Because God, infinite Intelligence, is perfect, whole, complete, and can never be added to nor taken from. God is all that is. God is the Reality which is limitless in every respect and is the Source of, and is in all things—the same yesterday, today, tomorrow, and forever. But flowing from this infinite and eternal sameness there is always endless change in the form and manner of expression and manifestation.

If we come to know that Life Itself is always the same in essence, including Its Law that governs Its expression, then we shall see that the manifestations of It in and as our experience would have to partake of Its consistent nature. Although Life goes forth into infinite forms of expression, It of Itself never changes. Suppose we could come to know that there is an order and symmetry in everything; that there is always enough love to go around, enough good, enough beauty, enough health and happiness, then we would know that everyone in the world could enjoy these things without ever exhausting their Source. Then we would have begun to grow up: to think logically; to realize that continued use of a basic principle never exhausts that principle. We can always add two and two and never deprive ourselves of the answer *four*. We need to have a big concept of the fundamental nature of Life, God, the Universe. We need to know there is a limitless abundance of all things good.

I knew a woman years ago who was despondent over her financial condition. She told me her affairs had continued to be chaotic until she realized something was wrong with her thinking. One day she went and sat on the beach—all day and nearly all night. She thought about how many grains of sand there are. She looked up and thought how many stars there are. She was so filled with thoughts of the abundance of nature with which she unified herself that she was able to change her former thinking then and there. Her experiences changed, too. How great is the view! We close it out when we put our little hands in front of our little eyes and refuse to look at things in a big way. We should identify ourselves with the infinite Presence that is universal and whose essence is our substance and supply. The biggest life is the one that includes the most.

God is One, not two. In this One, we are included, not excluded; for we are individualized centers in the Consciousness of God. Since there is only one final Person, God, we all live as personalities in that Person. This means that our personality is the use we are making of a Divine individuality that has been given us, the use we are making of our creative nature. If we wish an abundance of friendship and love, or of any good thing, we should think of the One Person in whom all people live. We should identify ourselves with God who is in every person.

But do we always do this? Do we expect an abundance of love and friendship, or do we deny it and say people don't like us? Of money, or of any other good thing, do we say that we don't know how it can be ours? There is One Source of everything in the universe, which takes the form of the supply we need when we need it. If in the process of the unfoldment of the supply we ought to meet people, we shall. There is but the One and we must go to the One. It is in us. It creates everything. It controls everything. It is everything. Jesus understood this. Therefore, he could find money in the fish's mouth, turn water into wine, multiply the loaves and fishes. But we have to start first with the Divine pattern. All the great thinkers and spiritual geniuses of the ages have believed this. It means that flowing through *me* is something akin to what is in *you*, but it also means we are free to choose and act upon our choices.

If I meet you as someone apart, someone I don't like or someone who doesn't like me, I am making a barrier between us. But if, turning away from everything that appears limited, we meet each other as Divine beings, this will also include us as humans. The greater will always include the lesser. We all have a certain kind of integrity which makes it almost impossible for us to violate, very consistently, that Something in us. Friendship begets friendship, love begets love, peace surrounds us with peace, joy creates joy, and a feeling of the abundance of everything in the universe automatically causes our adequate supply of all things to flow to us.

When this is not happening, what is choking it? Our own thinking! Not always our *conscious* thinking; for we seem to *want* all these things! It is more often an unconscious denial, or an objective appearance which provides a mental denial. This is why Jesus said: "Judge not according to the appearance . . ." The first thing we need to do is to get quiet within ourselves. Consciously deny any sense of fear and uncertainty, and consciously affirm the limitless abundance of God; until finally the unconscious or subjective reaction that had given rise to the reason why our good could not manifest no longer raises an argument. Whether we call this the argument of error or, as the psychologists say, the inertia of our thought patterns makes no difference. These thought patterns can be changed! Every time we identify ourselves with the Spirit within, we are dealing with a certainty, and every word of affirmation will replace a word of denial. In this way we build up within ourselves an acceptance of a greater good.

In order to illustrate this, let us consider the five fingers. There is a flow of blood from the heart down into and through them. If we were to strangulate that flow at the heart, none of the fingers would have any circulation. Let us say that we can never strangulate the heart, which we shall liken to the universal Spirit. It is always active. But down where the fingers are, there can be a strangulation in and about them so there is no circulation. We don't have to establish the stream of flow, but we do have to loosen the bands of fear that restrict the flow so that it will course through all five fingers. In other words, through some pattern of our thinking we strangulate the flow of Spirit, limiting abundance through many aspects of our lives.

There are in the world today approximately two billion three hundred million people. They are all supplied by the same spiritual life blood. They are all using the same Mind and living by the same Spirit. If something could remove every idea and concept of pestilence, famine, insecurity, and the fear we have of each other and of other nations, the Spirit would flow unobstructed. It would no longer be constricted by our sense of limitation. Someday this is going to happen. The only thing that will do it is a realization of the indwelling Spirit. We hear much about insecurity and the need to pray. There is a way of accepting the unlimited Life so that we shall no longer be afraid of ourselves. The only thing perpetuating fear is what Carl Jung calls the individual and collective thought patterns.

We must identify ourselves with the limitless Source of prosperity, love, friendship, happiness, and spontaneous joy, and maintain this identification through new and consistent patterns of thought. I like to be glad. I detest sadness. I know there is a lot of it in the world. I have had much of it, but I don't keep it very long. It is no good. Why should we have to go through life impoverished in a universe that is abundant in all things? Life is not just something to be endured. It is to be lived in joy, in a fullness without limit. We must get rid of old morbid theological concepts. I place no value on anything unless it brings gladness, love, friendship, the ability to laugh, and makes me feel that every person I meet, if I knew him, I would love. He is as good as I am, having the same heart pattern, the same kind of blood stream, the same Divinity.

Can there ever be a freedom of intellect or emotions, or the circulation of substance and supply in human experience until the Divine nature, the Source of all, is recognized and accepted without limitation? We struggle for the affection of two or three people to whom we give the power to destroy our happiness. Passing our doors are thousands who would love to embrace us. Isn't it strange? Yet we see it everywhere in life, the greater good held away because of a denial of the part. Or because we say there is only one avenue through which money or affection or appreciation can come, even though we are a part of and immersed in the limitless Source of such things. It is hard to grow up, isn't it? It is hard to gain spiritual maturity, to see that God is in everything.

The only thing that will release the strangulation hold we

have placed on our fuller experience of the unlimited abundance of all good things is for us to wake up mentally and emotionally. We need to escape from our old limited patterns of thinking and from our emotional anxieties and fears, and come to know the most practical thing in the world, the most dynamic truth: God is all there is, and in God there is no limitation. To the degree we stop limiting our thought of what God is, to that extent will we be able to enter a fuller experience of all that God is and can be in every aspect of our lives.

PART FOUR

The Power of Faith

All of science is based on the faith that the universe is lawful, logical, and orderly. It is a faith based on the reality of the invisible and intangible which is nevertheless the controlling and directive factor of the physical universe.

At the same time we have a similar faith in the power of the forces of Life to maintain and sustain us. Our heart beats, our blood circulates, our wounds heal. The unseen but ever-present power of Life is continually manifesting Itself in us. We have faith in It, but a faith not too consciously recognized. Yet, when recognized, the faith we have in Life's power to heal has brought forth amazing results.

A faith in the unseen, immeasurable creative powers of the Universe, in and through which all things are possible, is essential. Law does work, there is a beneficial purpose behind things, or nothing would exist. As we become aware of this we are able to develop faith to the point of a fine art and con-

stantly bring into our experience tangible expressions of the unseen creative Power which governs all.

In these chapters you will discover that you can develop a faith that cannot be shaken, and that it is a power that literally moves mountains.

13.

Faith, the Way to Life

CONVICTIONS HAVE POWER

Prayer, the desire to reach out to Something greater than we are, has been common to every age. Instinctively, we feel that there is a higher Power, a greater Intelligence, which responds to us. Our minds reach out with feeling and faith to a Something that is always available.

We need, and must have, a direct approach to Spirit. It is natural for us to reach out from our ignorance to Its enlightenment, from our weakness to Its strength, from our darkness to Its light. We feel and know that the Spirit is right where we are.

Every legitimate desire we have already has an answer in the Spirit, but it is faith or belief which causes It to respond to us. Faith not only lays hold of a Power which actually exists, it also causes this Power to respond as though It were a law operating for us. Somewhere along the line we shall have to surrender our weakness to Its strength, our fear to Its security, our lack to Its abundance. Everyone who has practiced faith knows this.

Why, then, shouldn't we consciously and definitely determine to develop such a faith? We need not ask *how* we should reach out to God, or by what authority, or under what name or sign. All we need do is *to reach*. God has made us all individuals; therefore, when each reaches in his own way he will be fulfilling the nature of his own being. No good can come from waiting until someone tells us just how, because his "just-how" could never be our "just-how." Every man will have to discover his own "just-how." And it will be right. It seems as though it would have to be direct and simple, personal and immediate, reaching out from our feeling of need with an equal feeling that the need will be met— reaching out with faith.

Let us believe in that Something bigger than we are, and come to trust It. It had intelligence enough to make everything, including ourselves; It governs by Law which controls everything, including ourselves. Why shouldn't we have an unlimited faith in It?

Jesus said that the very hairs of our head are numbered,

that not a sparrow falls to the ground without God knowing it. Would it not be wonderful to feel that we are cradled in such a Love and Wisdom? to know that Divine Power is immediately available to all of us? And now, because we need It so much, and because we feel we can no longer live without It, we are going to act as though It were right here, always responding to us, loving us in spite of our mistakes. Let's not be afraid to commune with this "Something" that is greater than we are.

Is not this the very essence of prayer? Just saying to Life, "Here I am. I let go of everything that does not belong to God's good man. I accept peace and comfort, today. And I desire to share with everyone I meet. God eternally forgives me as I discard all my weakness and uncertainty, all my past mistakes—I am no longer burdened by them. I know they are now lost in that greater experience of good which is now mine."

One of the tasks of the disciples was *to learn how to pray*. They had watched Jesus in his ministry among the sick and the ignorant, among those common people who heard him so gladly. They had seen new light come into the eyes of those whose vision had been dulled. They had seen a new energy flowing through the limbs of those who had been paralyzed. They had seen the lame walk, the dumb speak, and the deaf hear. And so the disciples asked him to teach them how to pray. Jesus answered them by saying that God was right where they were: ". . . behold, the kingdom of God is within you." He said that everyone who asks will receive. He said that everyone's method of prayer is good; that there is Something that answers everyone according to his belief in It; that God will never ask what you have been doing, or what mistakes you have made, or how good or bad you have been. When you ask, believing, He will give you what you ask for.

Jesus' words were so simple that we overlook their meaning: Something greater than I am, Something bigger, Something I can come to, Something that will listen, Something that understands, Something that will answer.

Next, Jesus gave the most simple prayer ever uttered, and the most effective. It is the only prayer common to all Christian faiths. Countless millions have been helped by it. Why shouldn't we? Perhaps, if we better understood its meaning, we should receive greater help through using it. What did Jesus mean when he said: "Our Father . . ."? That God is the Father of everyone—not just your Father, or my Father, but *our* Father. Being *our* Father, He is always ready to respond to us. We have a direct relationship to God, right now, while we are on this earth. Jesus said that we should come to this heavenly Father just as we would to an earthly one, tell Him what we need, and expect Him to provide a way through which our needs may be met. Jesus made the approach to God so very simple—*everyone's* Father, and *always available*. We couldn't ask for a closer relationship than this; he showed the relationship to be nearer than something outside us—as close to us as our very breath, as near as our hands and feet, for he said: "Our Father which art in heaven," and he had already told his disciples that *heaven is within*. He said, our Father is in heaven, and our heaven is already within, as well as around us. It is the Father within who doeth the works. We have no power of ourselves alone.

This is the relationship we have to God. This is the way we should feel when we commune with God, when we reach out to that Something greater than we are. And we should remember that reaching out is really reaching in, as well as out. If we were separated from God, how could we find Him? But if God has seen fit to implant His own Life in us, then He is as close to us as our thinking; and when we turn in thought to God, we are already communing with Him. Nothing could be more simple or more direct.

And now, according to this marvelous prayer, we are to turn within and find the Divine Presence which is greater than we are, greater than all people combined could possibly be—the one supreme, absolute, and perfect Power. *Our Father which art* means the Power that is, and *Our Father which art in heaven* means that this Power is within us and accessible to us.

Go inside yourself and you will meet God, right where you are, as what you are. The amazing thing is that every man is exactly where Jesus told him to go. He is there already. He does not have to go anywhere; he just begins right where he is. Jesus said we should go inside ourselves. He called this "entering the closet"—closing our eyes to everything outside and thinking and feeling something within. He said, when you have done this, very simply and directly, tell God just what you want.

The next thing he said is not quite so simple, for he added, when you tell God what you want, believe that He is going to give it to you. He was definite about this, for he said that when you ask God for something, you should believe not only that He is *going* to give it to you, but that he already *has given* it to you.

Can even God give us something we don't accept? The sun is shining, but we must step out of the shadow if we are to receive its rays. It all seems too good to be true, and yet, Jesus was able to prove what he was talking about. And it is only intelligent to believe someone who knows what he is talking about so well that he can really prove it. Jesus announced, with the utmost simplicity, that God is right where we are and responds to us; that He is greater than we are, and can and wants to help us; and that He will, when we believe He will.

So, every time we talk to God, let us affirm that God is giving us that which we ask and accept of Him.

14

An Experiment with Faith

DEVELOP YOUR POSSIBILITIES

We like to try out new things and see how they work. There wouldn't be much fun in living unless we did this, for life is a great adventure; as a matter of fact, is *the* great adventure. Unless new things are happening to us life becomes uninteresting and drab.

When God put us here He made each one of us just a little different, and if Divine Intelligence made each one of us just a little different, as though each one were a new mold, then the greatest adventure in life would be an experiment with ourselves to see what we could do with this thing that is within us.

We seem to be made up of flesh and blood and a hank of hair, a few clothes, and surrounded by certain conditions and situations. We seem to be the product of our environment. But this is a very superficial viewpoint. For while we are thinking of everyone as having just ordinary, commonplace talents, the first thing we know an Emerson or an Einstein appears, or a Buddha or a Jesus. And all the world marvels and says that they were not made of the same kind of stuff that you and I are made of.

This is where we make our biggest mistake, for in reality you will never discover anything outside you greater than you, yourself, are. Even the words and acts of the great mean nothing to us unless we can understand them. The things they say and do have no significance until we grasp their meaning. And we couldn't grasp their meaning unless there were something in us that is already equipped to seize on the truths they taught and make them our own.

When you go to hear a symphony, you don't go just to see others perform, or go to hear a great artist sing or a great musician play. What you really go for is that they awaken within you something that corresponds to and with what they are doing. And they really give you back to yourself. This, too, is an adventure in self-discovery.

Jesus turned water into wine. We believe that he did this because we believe that the Power of God was in him and it is the Power of God that makes the vine and the grape and the juice, and it is really the Power of God in nature that converts the juice into wine. Jesus changed this whole process and immediately converted water into wine because the Power that makes the wine and the water was already in him.

But suppose someone were to say to us: "Why don't you turn water into wine?" What would our response be? Well, we know what it would be—we would say: "Why, I can't turn water into wine. I wouldn't know how. The very idea is ridiculous." But how do we know that we couldn't turn water into wine? Who told us we couldn't? Perhaps we should think about the idea again and try to find out what it was that Jesus understood that enabled him to perform this miracle.

But someone may say: "Well, Jesus was different from other people." And maybe he was. But he didn't say that he was. As a matter of fact, he said, in effect, "What I am doing you can do too, if you actually believe in a Power greater than you are and come to know that you, as a human being, have nothing to do with the process of life whatsoever. You live but you did not create your own life. You think, but you didn't create your own mind. What you are is Spirit, but you didn't make that Spirit."

At once we are confronted with such a stupendous thought that it almost staggers the imagination: "There is Something in me greater than I appear to be, and that Something really isn't myself as a mere human being at all. It is

Something that was put there when I was born. There is a Presence and a Power within me waiting for my recognition. But a denial of them on my part makes it impossible for them to operate in a larger way. It is true that they are already working in me, in digesting my food, circulating my blood, causing my heart to beat, giving me such intelligence as I have. It is true that I didn't make any of these things.

"Perhaps I am asleep to the greater possibility. Perhaps I am as someone who is drugged and only half-conscious. If I could only wake up! If I could only believe that the Power which has done all this for me might be able to do a little more, perhaps It could do something beyond my wildest dream. How do I know? It told Einstein how to figure out his equations. It told Emerson how to write his essays. It told Browning how to write his poems. What happened to these people? They must have believed that they could do these things or they never would have attempted them."

And when we think of Jesus, the greatest of the great, perhaps when he first began to experiment with his faith, something said to him: "You can't multiply loaves and fishes. It is useless for you to tell the paralyzed man to get up and walk. There is no sense in your telling Lazarus to come forth from his tomb. You can't resurrect yourself."

How do we know but that early in life Jesus met the same difficulties we do, the same obstructions in his own mind?

He said that he had overcome the world; that he had conquered unbelief.

As a matter of fact, I think we would lose the whole meaning of his teaching, his life, and his work, if we overlook this. For certainly Jesus did not say, "I am more Divine than you are. God likes me better than He does you. God has told me secrets that He withholds from you." This is exactly what he never did say. Rather, he said, in effect, "I have overcome the world. I know that no man can take from or add to that which I am. I have come among you; I have lived with you and worked with you and taught you; I have told you about these things which I call the realities of the kingdom of heaven. And I am telling you that everything I do is an example of an adventure and an experiment you all may engage in with the same certainty, the same assurance."

And then he told them it was necessary for him to leave them, physically. They couldn't understand this for they were relying on him. He was the one who knew all the answers. He was the one who was close to God. He was their Saviour. But Jesus told them why it was necessary for him to depart from them, and I think he must have said something like this: "I have really been telling you about yourselves and somewhere along the line the Spirit of Truth within you, the Spirit of God in you, will reveal to you the meaning of everything I have said."

Jesus had finished the greatest experiment with life that any man ever made. There were no longer any questions or doubts, no longer any ifs or ands or buts. He implied: "This is the way it is. Now you prove it for yourselves."

Really, this is the adventure you and I are on. It is a terrific one and it should fire the imagination and the will to action. We are on the adventure of self-discovery through faith, and we are learning the greatest lesson in life—man doesn't live by bread alone but by a subtle Power which flows through everything, a Divine Presence which encompasses everything. Man doesn't live by will or wishing, or hope or longing. Man lives only because the Divine Life is his life.

God comes new and direct to everyone who expects Him, talks to everyone who listens, and acts through everyone who accepts His creativity. The authority or effectiveness of your word, your prayer, your meditation, rests in the action of the Law of God and not in you at all, just the same as the authority you have in the use of gravitational law and its response does not depend on you as a person. That authority is Divine; that authority is as absolute as you permit it to be. Our experiment is not with the Power or the Goodness or the Presence or the Love or the Truth or the Beauty of God, but with ourselves.

15

Dynamic Faith Is Effective!

IT CREATES YOUR EXPERIENCE

Did you ever say to yourself, "I wish that I might never again be afraid of anything"? Or have you met someone who had such a deep calm and peace that you have thought, "How I wish that I might be like that person"? Did you ever, in some still moment, feel as though you could almost reach out and touch something that would make you whole, happy, and complete?

I know you have, and I am sure everyone else has. We are all alike because we are all human beings. You share this feeling with every other person, and you instinctively know that there is something you ought to be able to tune in to which could make everything right, not only for yourself but for others and for the whole world.

What is the remedy for all this? Open your spiritual eyes! Listen with the inner ear! Open your minds!

What is it that you are to open your eyes, your ears, and your minds to? What is it that you must see, hear, and understand? It is this: Life flows into everything, through everything. It passes into every human event and translates Itself through every human act. If you learn to think of Life as flowing through your every action, you will soon discover that the things you give your attention to are quickened with new energy, for you are breathing the very essence of Being into them.

You can think yourself into being unhappy and depressed, or you can think yourself into being glad. Did it ever occur to you that you can also think yourself into being well? into being prosperous? that you can think yourself into success? Well, you can if you believe in the Law of Life, and use It rightly. But you must learn to use It affirmatively. You must learn to identify yourself with your desire.

You can use the laws of nature consciously and decide what you want them to do for you. You may have implicit confidence in them because you know they will never fail. You are surrounded by a Law of Mind which acts on your thought. This is the security of your faith and the answer to prayer.

You must become the master of your own thinking. This

is the only way you can realize freedom and joy. Therefore, you will have to turn your thoughts away from lack, want, and limitation, and let them dwell on good. *Make* yourself do this. Learn to think about what you wish to become.

You are a thinking center in Life, and the chief characteristic of the Law of Life is that It responds to thought. Your slightest thought sets up a pattern which is acted upon by Creative Intelligence, causing to be created for you circumstances which will correspond to your thought.

If you think of Life as always bringing to you everything you need, you will have formed a partnership with the Invisible which will prosper you in everything you do. If you think of the organs and functions of your body as activities of Life, then automatically you will be benefited physically.

The spiritual gifts which people have so earnestly sought after are not something that God has withheld from man. Quite the reverse. They are something which man, in his ignorance, has withheld from himself. Life is not vindictive; It is not withholding anything from you.

If you will take time daily to sense the presence of Life within you, to believe in It, to accept It, it will not be long before undesirable experiences which you have known will gradually disappear and something new will be born—a bigger, better, and more perfect you. You will pass from lack and want into greater freedom; from fear into faith. From a sense of being alone, you will pass into the realization of a Oneness with everything, and you will rejoice.

There may be some who think that before they can achieve this they must become profound philosophers, spiritual sages, or men of such deep scientific knowledge that they stand apart from the rest of the world. This is not true. What the wisest have known is only a little more than you and I know. They cannot answer your questions for you; you will have to answer them for yourself. Even the best man who ever lived could not live for you; you will have to live for yourself.

You are some part of God, whether or not you know it or believe it; but you may have hypnotized yourself into thinking that you are incomplete and imperfect and identified yourself with the fantastic pictures of your morbid dreams. But the ropes that bind you are as ropes of sand.

To understand that your faith is operated on by a natural law gives you the key to the situation. But it is not enough just to believe in a principle. This is only the starting point. Principles have to be used if they are going to produce definite results for you, and whether the principles are physical, mental, or spiritual makes no difference.

It is not enough to say that faith can do anything, for most people already believe this. What you have to do is not only to realize that faith *can* do things, you have to find out how faith is acquired and then you have to *use* it for definite purposes.

To merely state that you believe that God is all there is will not necessarily cause anything to happen. But when you believe that God is all there is, and when you have implicit confidence in the Law of Good, and when you use this belief for a definite purpose, then something will happen. And the reason why it happens is that you are surrounded by a creative Power—or a creative Mind, or a creative Principle, whatever you choose to call it—which actually does respond according to your thinking. This is the key to the whole situation.

Learn to make known your requests with thanksgiving and in acceptance. And having done this, in that silent communion of your soul with its Source, believe that the Law of Good will do the rest.

If, then, you can come to see that such a Law exists and that you are using a Power greater than you are, you will at once be relieved of any sense of responsibility about it as though you had to make the Law work. For you do not sit around holding thoughts or trying to compel things to happen. As a matter of fact, this would defeat the very purpose you wish to accomplish. You can no more make the Law of Mind creative than you can compel an acorn to become an oak. You do not hold thoughts over the acorn nor do you visualize an oak tree. What you do is plant an acorn and let nature create the oak tree for you.

You are in partnership with the Giver of all life—God, the living Spirit, almighty and ever present. Therefore, say to yourself quietly but with deep conviction:

I now accept my Divine birthright. I now consciously enter into my partnership with love, with peace, with joy, with God. I feel the infinite Presence close around me. I feel the warmth, the color, and the radiance of this Presence like a living thing in which I am enveloped.

I am no longer afraid of life. A deep and abiding sense of calm and of poise flows through me. I have faith to believe that the kingdom of God is at hand. It is right, where I am, here, now, today, at this moment.

I feel that there is a Law of Good which can, will, and does govern everything. Therefore, I feel that everything in my life is constructive, everything in my thought that is life-giving is blessed and prospered. It blesses everyone I meet. It makes glad every situation I find myself in. It brings peace and comfort to everyone I contact. I am united with everything in life in love, in peace, and in joy. And I know that the Presence of Love and Life gently leads me and all others, guiding, guarding, sustaining, upholding, now and forever.

16

The Use of Spiritual Ideas

When we say there is a Power greater than we are, we are talking about a spiritual Power everybody can use, if he believes in It. Someone may say this is nonsense; but stop to think a moment. Every time you plant a garden you use a Power greater than you are. No one living knows how to make a plant or a tree; no one living knows how a chicken gets in an egg, or an egg in a chicken. We are three-dimensional beings living in a four-dimensional world which governs the three-dimensional. We do not have to try to explain the inexplicable.

There is a Power in the universe greater than we are—an Intelligence acting as Law that receives the impress of our thought as we think it. It is creative and It always tends to create for us the conditions we think about and accept. And if we wish to help someone else through our prayer or spiritual mind treatment, It will create for the person whom we identify with It. We don't have to worry whether somebody else believes or not. We should only be concerned about what we believe and then demonstrate it.

People sometimes ask me if it is spiritual to pray for material things. There is no such thing as a strictly material universe. Science has outgrown such a material concept; there can be no material universe separate from the spiritual Reality that governs and molds it. There is a Power greater than we are and everything that is visible is an expression of It. All things come forth from It and all things are contained in It, and we are in It and It responds directly to us personally at the level of our conviction that It is responding.

Someone might ask why does not the Power force conviction and faith upon us? It does not force anything upon anyone. Does a garden produce carrots when we plant beets? We have been so afraid of a vengeful God, thinking that we are made to suffer here so that we will suffer less hereafter, that we are all mixed up in our ideas about our relationship to the Infinite. There are certain laws we have to obey on the physical level, and it is the same with spiritual law as it is with physical law, only spiritual law is on a higher level. The laws work just the same.

For instance, there is a law of attraction and repulsion in mind that works just like attraction and repulsion in physics—it always tends to provide for us that which is like our own thinking. Whatsoever things are lovely and of good report, *think on these things,* the Bible says. As a man thinketh in his heart so is he; believe, and it shall be done unto you—this is the secret. There is a principle that responds to us creatively at the level of our own consciousness. To the pure in heart all will be pure. To the ones who see that everything is wrong, everything will be wrong. The ones who criticize everything and everybody will always find something to criticize. But we know that they are trying to justify themselves, they are afraid of themselves, they don't believe in themselves. They have a sense of guilt and rejection and an anxiety and an insecurity within themselves, therefore they are sick. In this sense we are sorry for them, but there is no reason why you and I should have to be like them.

There is no reason to suppose that God is some sad Creature sending thunderbolts to Methodists and candy to Baptists. The Universal loves all of us; It is impartial. There is nothing in nature or in God that withholds our good from us. There is nothing in the universe that keeps us waiting until we "get saved." You and I believe in a Power greater than we are and we believe It is Good; we believe It is Love, Truth, and Beauty. We believe It responds to us, and if we

maintain a certain mental attitude of thought It will automatically bring to us those things that make life happy. Life
ought to be happy; there is no "weeping" God, of this I
am sure.

We believe in something so wonderful that at first it
seems impossible, yet it is so practical that it touches every
moment of our lives. If we can get rid of all the thoughts
that say to us we are hurt, sensitive, and unwanted—
without being mean or arrogant about it—we shall no longer be hurt or led into situations where people will wish to
hurt us. It is just as though all that God is is personal to each
one of us. Isn't all the law of mathematics right at the finger
tips of the mathematician when he is using it? Isn't all the
harmony there is available to the one who sings? All of gravity is holding everything in place, as though all of gravity
devoted its entire attention and effort to holding a peanut
right where I might put it.

We meet God in ourselves and in each other and in nature and everywhere. But how can we understand a God of
Love if we are looking at life with hate? How can we accept
a God of Abundance if we think only of impoverishment?
How can we experience a life of harmony if we are always in
discord? There seems to be a certain psychological morbidity about all of us. In the background is the idea that if we
suffer in this world then we shall go to a good place after-

wards. Actually, *that* which is the Reality comes fresh, new, clean, beautiful, lovely, exhilarant, majestic, dynamic, omnipotent to each one of us every moment of our time. *That* which is the original creative Intelligence, *that* which is alive with Life and aflame with Love is right at the point of our inner listening, right at the point of our envisioning. This is the way it is. We did not make it this way, but we can thank God that each one of us has access to the infinite and ineffable All.

It all is as obvious as planting sunflower seeds and getting sunflowers. Jesus understood this—kind for kind. We cannot jump off a cliff and expect the law of gravitation to suspend its action just those few moments for us. We do not expect the laws of nature to disobey themselves to please the scientist; but somehow when we come to mental or spiritual things we expect the whole order of the universe to reverse itself, that out of the chaos and confusion of our thought we should be able to have an experience of peace and happiness.

It is fundamental to our wholeness and to our well-being that we must learn to affirm what we desire. We must learn to enthusiastically expect those things of good which we wish to experience. Everyone can pray an affirmative prayer; and we do not have to wonder if the Law of Mind will operate for us. It cannot help it as It acts by reflection. As we

Ernest Holmes

advance in our demonstrations of this most fascinating of all sciences we shall discover that the only way to change the outer condition is by inwardly changing the nature of our thought, which is then reflected as the condition.

We must remember, too, that we carry around the thought habit patterns of the ages. But we may be sure that there is a spiritual integrity within us such as we shall discover nowhere outside ourselves. Here we shall meet life; here decide that we may neutralize negative thought patterns by denying them; here accept the Power greater than we are, knowing that no matter what our mistakes It holds nothing against us—ever. Our part is really to wipe the slate of the past clean of fear and doubt and unloveliness and write a new song of acceptance of Life and Love, knowing that they forever hold us in their embrace.

Let us no longer be morbid over the past, nor afraid of the present, nor insecure about the future; but, looking in, up, and out, let each see himself as a Son who knows he is beloved of God.

PART FIVE

How to Live Successfully

Properly viewed, we are always successful in all things. That is, we always seem to experience the ideas which dominate our thought, regardless of what those ideas may be. They could be of accomplishment or failure, it doesn't matter, for if we have had a fulfillment in our experience of what we have thought about most, then we have been successful.

There is always a logical sequence of cause and effect. We cannot expect our experience to be different from the mental patterns we have established for it. We cannot be healthy if we constantly think of illness, neither can we possess wealth if we let our thoughts dwell on poverty. There is a definite correlation between thought and experience which nothing can violate.

To change an experience from bad to better, we change our thinking about that experience, establishing thought patterns *of what we want rather than what we don't want. Successful attainment of better experiences in living depends on the manner in which we are able to manage our thinking.*

These closing chapters can show you the way to a better life than you have yet dreamed of.

17

The Way to Succeed

THERE ARE DEFINITE RULES

There are needs which the human mind has and which every man has in common; one of them is the need for success. I would like to develop the reason why I believe this to be so.

Science of Mind is a practical philosophy. It is based on the wisdom and deep abstract concepts of the ages but never departs from an intelligent perspective of life and gives us a great latitude for personal action. We believe that there is only One Mind in the universe, One ultimate Self or Spirit, and we live in It and by It. We believe that all law is an activity of this Intelligence. The Bible tells us that "In the beginning was the Word, and the Word was with God, and the Word was God. . . . All things were made by him; and without him was not any thing made that was made." God is all—God is everywhere—God is everything.

Throughout the ages people have prayed, and we believe all prayers have been answered in such degrees as they have been consistent with the nature of Reality. We function in or manifest God's Mind at the level of our individual perception. There is at the center of your being and of mine an inner Presence always seeking a greater expression of Itself.

Now we believe that we can sit in the silence of our own thought, give a treatment, say a prayer, affirm something, or accept something, and as a result of what we do mentally something happens in our experience. This does not mean that our thought causes something to happen, but rather that we have permitted something to happen by the action of a Power greater than we are flowing through it.

We have to understand what the wise and the good have always taught: The universe is a living system of intelligence, will, imagination, and freedom, but always acting in accord with law. There seems to be no other explanation of life and the world as we know it. Whenever a prayer has been answered it has been answered according to our belief in it and through a corresponding action of law.

There is within us, now, the possibility of greatness, the possibility of limitless success in life. There is nothing unspiritual about this concept, for you and I live in God, by God, and with God. Whatever the ultimate Power of the universe is, It is One; and since It is One It is undivided, therefore It is here. Since It is here, It is where we are and what we are within ourselves, and only within ourselves shall we discover God. That is why Emerson said we cannot be satisfied except by the triumph of principle that is within our own mind. There is no division, no separation; God is Life as well as Law.

You and I always have immediate access to God. We may always initiate a new cause, a new pattern of thought, decree a thing and have it happen, providing it is in line with the nature of Reality. Our thought as prayer cannot make the world become flat, it can only flatten our experience of it. Our thought has to be naturally consistent with the Law of God. We do not have to accept dogmatic statements about this, instead we must prove it for ourselves.

There is only one human race; one heart beats in every human breast. Back of you and back of me, however inadequate we may appear, is the potential of the Infinite, surging through us to express as life, truth, action—as successful living. There is no law of God that deprives us of experiencing a greater degree of His nature. I do not believe the Infinite could possibly impose limitation on Its creation without limiting Itself, which of course would be impossible. But I believe we are all coming up through ignorance to a greater enlightenment.

Jesus, the most exalted of all the great teachers and prophets the world has ever known, stated simply and most effectively a principle we are always consciously or unconsciously using: ". . . as thou hast believed, so be it done unto thee." He implied there is something that responds to our belief *the way we believe it.*

In this concept rests the idea that we experience what we accept. However, we do not say to someone, "You must believe this, too, because we believe it." We should not believe something just because someone else believes it. It is not what you and I believe that makes truth; but we are fortunate if what we believe is truth, for then all the Power of heaven and earth is allied with us. Sitting quietly, announcing that God is all there is, each may say, no matter what the present appearance may be, "Good and only good shall come to me."

There is nothing in the outer world that can attach itself to us unless we mentally attach ourselves to it first—in ignorance as a rule. We are held in bondage until we consciously seek the enlightenment that sets us free. Successful living has nothing to do with mental suggestion; it has to do with inward knowing. To know is to experience. There is no other way to be certain. Until you and I realize that we can decree the thing and then experience it, we shall not understand the only real security there is in the universe. Times may change, people may come and go, but the One who changeth not abides with us eternally. We are immersed in a living Presence which is God, personal to each one of us. You and I must come to know God as an immediate experience and as always creatively active in our lives.

I find nothing in logic or reason to contradict this idea. We have this need of God, this need of consciously feeling the warmth and color, the action and intelligence and enthusiasm of the Universal at the center of our own being. Some people are so used to thinking of a reluctant God doling out gifts that it is hard for them to understand that to have prayer be effective they must believe the prayer is answered when they pray it. But time and experience have proved this to be true to millions of people. Something responds to us the way we believe. God is real.

We must come at last to believe in our own word of affirmation and acceptance; not only to put our hope into words, but also to accept the realization of that hope. Any person who will do this consistently, who will continue to announce his good and to believe in it, most surely will find the seeming barren areas of his life awaken to new creativity. To keep an integrity with our own soul, to trust our-self though all men doubt us, yet "make allowance for their doubting, too," is to let go of all that denies the magnificence and beneficence of God. It is to lay down the fear of the unknown and to take up the challenge of confidence in the Invisible, and to consciously place our hand in the hand of the Infinite, accepting the love and light and truth and peace that is at the center of our being.

So shall we find that our word ever accomplishes that which is good and always prospers that thing whereto we direct it.

18.

How to Build Security

Everyone is looking for security, and often we think the word "security" means that we have money enough to pay the bills. It does certainly include that. But there is a deeper security than that, a security that comes only through a deep and abiding faith in Life; a deep and abiding faith in ourselves, and a deep and abiding faith in God. There is no security in life without this faith. That is why a person is not healed of a neurosis without attaining some kind of new faith. There is no permanent healing of anything in life without a restoration of faith. There is no gratification or feeling of safety without faith. Why is this so? I do not know, but I have a theory about it.

My theory is very simple. Every man is on the pathway

of an endless evolution. There is Something that impels him; there is a spark of Divinity that shapes his ends, rough hew them though he may, as Shakespeare said. Everyone has an urge to live, to sing, to dance, to accomplish something, to love something, and to give. The moment we stop the loving and the giving we are forlorn—we are unhappy.

I think we belong to God, we are *of* God, the very essence of God. Spirit, I believe, is incarnated in everything and in everyone. There is only One Spirit, but innumerable incarnations. We are, as Browning said, a God though in the germ. I am sure millions of people hold this view, but not everyone understands it, or they do not think about it enough. If we are not willing to think, we are wasting our time. Think! Someone said, "Keep faith with reason for she will convert thy soul."

It is unreasonable and illogical to suppose that the supreme Life would create something that It could destroy. When Jesus was asked about God's relationship to the dead, he answered as we would expect an inspired spiritual genuis to answer: "God is not the God of the dead, but of the living . . . for all live unto him." Now that is logical; it is rational and reasonable and sound. God is Life, and cannot produce death. God is Peace, and cannot produce confusion. God is Love, and cannot produce fear. You and I have to come to believe this if we would know security.

You see God has entered into you and me. We could not find anything in us that is really separated from God, except our belief. We seem to have that freedom. And if this is true, how can we hope to have security unless that security is based on our own unity with God, on our own Divinity? "Hear, O Israel; The Lord thy God is one Lord." There is only One. That is why Emerson said that "there is one mind common to all individual men."

Your mind is God's Mind in you, as you. Your spirit is the Spirit of God in you, as you. This you did not make. *It is*, and will not be changed. This is the great secret that Jesus taught, as have all of the other great teachers of man. In essence no race, no person, no form of life is external to our own. We cannot exclude any facet of life and have a universe left. We will only have a fragment of a universe in which we will blindly stumble around.

God is our life *now*. It is not a life that we are going to attain some day. It *is* our life. We are not gradually becoming unified with God; we cannot be separated from God! We shall never have to unify with God, but we shall have to recognize that we are not separated from God. Then, that in our experience which appears to be separated will flow together; it will rush together, as the mountain torrent rushes across the valley to join the ocean of its infinitude.

There is Something in you and in me that foreknows

these things; no one taught us or caused us to remember that celestial palace whence we came. But how can we hope to have a sense of security if we separate ourselves in belief from That which alone can give it? Who hath power to give us life but God? Science cannot bestow it. The various branches of learning are fine and wonderful, but they do not give us life—they only tell us about it. There is no security unless we have a deep and abiding faith in Life; a faith which permits Life to flow through us, but only at the level of our understanding and acceptance of It.

What inhibits It? We pretty well know now. We are born with a desire to love, to laugh, to sing, to dance, to create. Without being technical about it, we are born with an emotional craving for self-expression. Life is action, movement, and enthusiasm. Unless we keep doing new things, we will not have the interest to do new things. This is the secret of growing up mentally, emotionally, and spiritually. We shall never recapture yesterday, we shall never catch up with tomorrow for it eludes us; but today is ours! This day in which we live, this hour, this moment is one from which we should distill all the joy there is, all the enthusiasm.

Do you know that people who are unenthusiastic are always tired? It is now definitely known that, unless there is a physical infection, most weariness is associated with ennui which comes psychologically and emotionally because the individual isn't interested in others, or in living. It is definitely known that those who stop living for others, stop living. The emotional energy, which is the greatest creative force we have, is designed to go out and express itself in wholesome action. This energy is as real as the energy of physics. If it is inhibited it still remains in a dynamic state and the result is a discharge of energy in what we know as an inner conflict or complex.

I believe that everything that exists is an expression of God, and that is why we are here. There is an inner Something in man that belongs to the Universe and we have to get rid of all that inhibits It—every sense of rejection and guilt and insecurity and anxiety. The security I am talking about is the kind that not only warms the heart and makes glad the mind, but feeds the soul. We belong to God. There is That within us which will last forever. "I am That which Thou art." There is no other security.

What joy we would have if we would just see God in each other and in human events! If we know God is our substance, we shall have supply. If we know God is our friend, we shall have friends. If we love everybody, there will be enough people to return that love to us. This is security, and there is no peace of mind not based on this security. There is no final peace but love; there is no final security anywhere in the universe but a faith in Life that proves itself. Truth demonstrates itself without effort. We are begirt by spiritual laws which execute themselves, as Emerson said.

So there must be a deep sense of love and givingness if we are going to have a real security and peace of mind. There is in us a primal Cause, an ultimate Reality, a cosmic Wholeness, a God from whom all things flow and in whom all things move and live.

We are not all of God, of course, but everything that we are is made out of God because there is nothing else it can be made of. The Universe holds us forever in Its warm and close embrace. When you and I turn to that Divinity within us we shall feel something and we shall know something which every endeavor of the ages has sought after—the living God. Engraved on the scroll of the Universe is the inextinguishable imprint of our own individuality—the name of the beloved Son.

Here and here alone is security; here and here alone is peace. But not in splendid isolation shall it be found. It is in the wind and the wave, the song of the child, the crooning of the mother, the beauty of the sunset, and the golden glory of dawn's rise over the mountaintops flinging its light into the newness of another day. It is not just in religious adoration, but in the stillness of our own heart that He speaks.

Thought and Physical Health

Your Body Reflects Your Ideas

S cience of Mind is a real science, a practical, workable
science which can be taught to and understood and
used by anyone. It is the newest of all sciences and the most
effectual.

In Science of Mind we do not deny that people are sick.
We do not have to deny one truth to affirm another. We
believe in the application of medicine, surgery, sanitation,
diet, proper exercise—everything that belongs to the plane
or the level upon which the various aspects of life function.
It has been my endeavor to make Science of Mind a bridge
between the world of experience and the indwelling Spirit,
between what ails us and what can make us well, and this
includes psychosomatic medicine and the physician. We are

the first metaphysical group that has ever recognized the wholeness and unity of all things and that is why there are so many leading physicians and surgeons who adhere to and use the principles of Science of Mind.

We believe that man is a spiritual being right now, living in a spiritual universe right now, and that every man is an incarnation of God—right now! All of the Power and Presence, all of the Wholeness in the universe is available to man right now. There is nothing but God. I believe the time will come when this idea will be taught from the kindergarten level on up.

There is a spiritual man who never gets sick; if he did, neither medicine, surgery, nor prayer could heal him. There is nothing you and I can do objectively, subjectively, or spiritually to change *the nature of God*. ". . . the Lord he is God: there is none else beside him."

The ancient Chinese said that man has three bodies; a physical, a mental, and a spiritual body. It was believed that his physical body could not be well unless there were circulation. It was only about three hundred years ago that the circulation of the blood was discovered. We now know that there must be circulation, assimilation, and elimination if there is going to be physical health. The ancient Chinese recognized that where there is no circulation there is stagnation, infection, and death. But they also said that man has a mental body and that there can be no physical circulation that is right unless the mental circulates through the physical.

It is within the memory of all of us that there was first introduced the idea of what is now called psychosomatic medicine—psyche meaning mind, and soma meaning body, therefore, we have psychosomatic meaning mind-body relationship. This is a recent thing with us; but the ancient Chinese said there must be a circulation of the mental body through the physical body because they are so closely allied—the very core, sinew, flesh, and blood of psychosomatic medicine. It is believed today that from seventy-five to ninety percent of all ailments and diseases are unconsciously invoked by some mental or emotional action.

And the Chinese also said that there not only must be a circulation of the mental through the physical, but there also must be a circulation of the spiritual through the mental because man has a spiritual body and the mental body cannot circulate through the physical until the spiritual has circulated through the mental. The Bible reminds us that man is spirit.

In Science of Mind we do not deny the physical or the mental, but we say there is also the spiritual. This is our field of therapeutics: We say that man's body is the instrument of his mind or consciousness, but that his mind is at the same time the instrument of his spirit—". . . there is a spirit in man: and the inspiration of the Almighty giveth them understanding."

Future generations will be taught the need of quiet contemplation that they may sense and realize the Presence of God in their minds, in the activities within their bodies, and in their affairs. Let us think about this. We can heal ourselves of most of our physical troubles if we go about it rightly, and we can heal others just as well. We should not think that we have to wait for some spiritually enlightened person to come along or until we attain the ultimate in maturity ourselves.

Jesus was a man who knew God and I think the greatest thing he ever said was, "Neither do I condemn thee." The older I grow, the more I realize that human kindness is the greatest quality on earth. I sense the depth and breadth, and feel the height and wonderful illumination of the man who could say that. But Jesus was also a man of justice for he warned that making the same mistake again would result in the same consequence. The Universe is just without judgment. This is a terrific concept!

All disease is unnatural and does not belong to the *real* person—if it did, no one could heal it. Any doctor will tell you it is the nature of the body to heal itself of every disease, and that it is the nature of the mind to fight off every psychosis and neurosis. If they didn't, no one could be healed. There is no physician who thinks he heals anything or anyone. He only assists nature in re-establishing the normal processes of circulation, assimilation, and elimination in both body and mind.

You and I deal with spiritual mind healing. We believe in the practice of spiritual meditation consciously used for definite healing purposes. We not only believe in it, we know it is true. While we gratefully acknowledge the contribution that is made in every field to alleviate suffering, we do believe in a *transcendence*. We believe there is a Power beyond the physical and beyond the intellect and that It is spiritual. Now, what do we mean by a spiritual Power?

"Shew us the Father, and it sufficeth us," said Philip. "Jesus saith unto him, Have I been so long time with you, and yet hast thou not known me, Philip? he that hath seen me, hath seen the Father. . . ." Jesus was talking about the spiritual man. There is in everyone this spiritual man, this Christ, Atman, Buddha—it does not matter the name we give it. This is the Son begotten of the only Father, and each is that Son right now. "Know ye not that ye are the temple of God, and that the Spirit of God dwelleth in you?"

Spiritual thinking means the realization and affirmation that God is all there is. When we properly identify ourselves with this ultimate Perfection we realize that there is a necessity for us to experience perfect circulation, perfect assimilation, and perfect elimination through our physical body as well as through the body of our affairs.

Each is his own best practitioner, his own best physician, because the Spirit within us is God. It knows all things, sees all things, hears all things, understands all things because It is all things. Therefore, spiritual mind healing means that we identify our consciousness with the One Mind, the Mind that is God. The greatest trouble we have in our work is to convince people that what they are looking for, they are looking with; that the God they are trying to become good enough to understand *is* at the center of their being now, and that the creative word they want to use is the word they *are* using. Though for the most part they use it unconsciously and deny their good instead of accepting it.

If we have to find a good power with which to combat a bad power, where would we go to get it? If my soul were lost, would you know where to look for it? How well Jesus knew this. Emerson knew it also for he said "stay at home with the cause." We have to be still and come to know that we are the manifestation of God. We have a spiritual body right now that is perfect, that is not lame or sick, that does not hurt nor is congested, that has no disease. If we did not have it, neither psychology, medicine, nor metaphysics could help us. All in the world any of us can do is to *adjust that which we seem to be to that which we really are!* Jesus called this knowing the truth. "And ye shall know the truth, and the truth shall make you free."

There is a Spirit in us that bears witness to the truth. Though we may not look it, and often may not act it, we are *perfect* right now. The knowledge and use of this truth of being will make us free of the limitations that our ignorance has brought upon us.

If one has a pain it should be relieved, because it is foolish to think that God wants us to suffer. That is ignorance. We, therefore, do not deny that hospitals are needed as well as doctors and surgeons and nurses. But isn't it wonderful that the great Physician is right where we are, always? Always ready to be called upon by either ourselves or the medical man.

This is the most difficult thing to teach. Nine out of ten people think a spiritual mind treatment is something different from what it is and has to be: the recognition that man's life is some part of God. Jesus knew this and taught over and over that "the kingdom of God is within," that each is a Son of the Most High in whom there is no condemnation. We must come to know the *self* that each is and must be. Then will the glory of this eternal *self* spill itself into the desert of our hopelessness, warm the creative soil of our mind, and flow through our thought into our body in words immaculate.

It is so very simple! There is perfect circulation, there is perfect assimilation, there is perfect elimination, for there is no congestion and no limitation in the Divinity at the center of our being! We should glory and delight in it.

Perhaps some of you are asking yourselves, "What words shall I use?"

Use the words that mean something to you, because the word is a mold for the living essence, making it vibrant with life. Any word that means freedom to you will produce freedom.

Some of you might be saying, "How do I really know enough to speak such words?"

Did not Jesus point to a little child and say "of such is the kingdom of God"? A child is eager to learn, willing to believe, trusting, his imagination is alive and vital. We have to become teachable all over again if we are to learn to experience a finer, higher concept of life.

One of the main efforts in modern medicine is to show individuals that their thoughts are the principal causes of their physical problems; and that once they learn to avoid thinking in a manner that inhibits the natural normal flow of Life through the body it readily returns to a state of health. The body has its roots, its source, its pattern in a spiritual world—in the nature of God which is perfect. But we seem to go out of our way to maintain ideas and thoughts contrary to this perfection which in turn prevents it from being manifested in and through our body and our affairs. Healthful living is available for us to experience when we re-educate ourselves to think in terms of health rather than of illness.

This applies to the entire realm of thinking. Every thought has some effect and helps shape our experience. Our great freedom is that we may choose our thoughts! We need to begin to think anew about ourselves and our relationship to God. Let us practice the principle of beholding our Divine Sonship in ourselves, and in all others as well, until it makes its appearance in all of our relationships. Too long have we misinterpreted life in words of hate and condemnation, of fear and limitation.

There is a perfect spiritual body which is a part of everyone's Divine heritage. No matter through what other avenues we may seek to meet our physical and mental needs, let us often sit in the silence of our own soul in adoration of the inner Spirit. Let us in consciousness revere the God who never did anything wrong. More often than we have ever done, let us in our thought and feeling say, "Holy, holy, holy, Lord God Almighty within me." Let us surrender the littleness of human conceit and pride and fear and injustice. It can be done, for there is no mediator between ourselves and the eternal Reality.

Remember this: Any word you speak with meaning will have power. Do not try to use words I write, the words of other writers, or even words that are in the Bible. They are good, but the word that springs spontaneously in your own heart and mind is the right word to use in prayer or treatment.

Let us believe as we have never believed before in the imprisoned splendor within ourselves, loosed by our own words. It is God who has willed it, the Law of God establishes it, and our experiences may demonstrate it. The Source of all the good we have so earnestly sought out, we have with us. Our health, our permanent well-being, lie in our realization of our eternal and ineffable life in God. In Him we live and move and have our being; but we must deny everything that denies this and affirm that which establishes it.

Is it not wonderful to know that that which the prophets have prophesied, that which the sages have taught and the poets have written about is true? The more exalted the thought and emotion, the statelier mansions we build. We shall leave the "low-vaulted past" as we build each "new temple, nobler than the last." Let us use our imagination and will and feeling in prayerful attitude and think about God being that which we are, until every mental and emotional congestion is loosened and let go in the acceptance of the glory of something transcendent which comes to us. As we *know* this the body responds, for it is immersed in Something superior to itself.

We are so One with the Whole that what is true of It is also true of us. Life is forever taking form in us. The entire order is one of spontaneous being and spontaneous manifestation. The Law follows the word just as the word follows the desire. This creative process goes on whether we agree that it does or not. Our experiences will change when we purposefully desire to change them for the better.

Going forth into the early morn of a day of new hope, forgetting the old, rising above the doubt and fear of yesterday, let us dare to believe that today there comes into our consciousness something new, something noble, something transcendent, which sings to us of a joy ineffable, of a God approachable, of a hope realized, of a life lived in wholeness.

You Are Immortal, Now!

THERE IS ONLY ONE LIFE

There are three ways in which the human mind gathers knowledge, so far as is now known. One is by science, which is the knowledge of the laws of nature. Another is by intuition, which includes revelation, inspiration, and all religions. The other way is philosophy, which contains all of the opinions of the ages—what is right or wrong, what is rational, what is logical, what is reasonable. We are interested now in finding the contributions that these different avenues make to our acceptance of immortality.

Every great religion has believed in the immortality and the ongoingness of the soul. The whole system of the ancient Hindus was built on the idea that God—Reality, Truth, Brahma—is only *One*, beside which there is none other, and that every one of us is an incarnation of It; that we are gradually unfolding or evolving into all of It, that It flows through every one of us. We belong to the Christian faith which is a combination of the old Hebrew idea that God speaks from without, and the Greek idea that God speaks from within. We say the highest God and the innermost God is One God.

Now we do not want to believe in immortality simply because somebody became immortalized through the resurrection, which I believe in easily enough. Jesus, I believe, became resurrected to prove the eternality of the soul. You and I are given life, inherent, and we cannot live by proxy. It does not matter how good Jesus was, or how saintly Buddha was, or how great a man one of the ancient Hindus must have been, there is that within each of us which must bear witness to every truth, to every fact, and to every experience; and until it does we are only half-being, half-hearing, and half-knowing. Can someone else play a game for you? If you feel like weeping, can you get somebody to cry for you, real tears? Can somebody else love for you? Of course not! We must meet life individually, as well as collectively, and only the man who does is at peace. It is only in our own integrity that we shall ever see God. We cannot live and be whole because somebody else was a good man. Jesus knew this. He said: "Why callest thou me good? there is none good but one, that is, God." And he called God "the Father, that dwelleth in me." When they wanted to make him a king he said, in effect, that it was expedient that he go away, so that the Spirit of Truth should bear witness to the Divine fact of our own being.

We find Socrates, who was called the Father of Philosophy, and Kant, who was called the Father of Reason, both teaching that God is One and that we are a part of Him. Logic would tell us that there cannot be two infinites—there can only be one finality in the universe. Logic also would tell us how futile it would be if "six feet under and all is over." What an economic waste of energy and time! How irrational the Universe would be! Emerson said we are organs of the Infinite. There is incarnated in each of us that Divine spark which is of the nature of God, and, carrying us through the process of evolution, gradually unfolds until we are so unified with Him that you cannot tell where the one begins and the other leaves off. It is the nature of the Father to be inherent in the Son.

Now let us see what science can tell us about immortality. It is now held by some scientists that there is not an atom of our physical body that was in it a short time ago, some say eleven months; but in any event, no one is over a year old as far as the physical composition of his body is concerned. But we do not all look that young, of that I am sure.

At the same time, many leading psychologists hold that the mind cannot wear out, although it may appear to become confused. This is interesting, isn't it? What is back of it? Not somebody's opinion, not some sin and salvation theory, not someone's theology, but certain scientific truths, certain universal realities, certain laws of our own being that we ought to consider. Too often our faith must be propped up every few moments, and unless we arrive at a conviction beyond that kind of need, we shall always be exclaiming, "Lord, I believe; help thou mine unbelief."

Behind the thought that the body is not over a year old is another thought: Everything in the universe is in a state of continual flux; new substances appearing all the time—the old disappearing, giving place to the new in all creation. If this is true of our physical body, we have no reason to doubt that it may be true of the structure of the whole physical universe, and that back of it is that Life which forevermore makes everything new. This is not a wild phantasy. God is not old or young, but without birth and without death, and we live and move and have our being in this eternal sea of never-ending Life.

Why is it that the mind cannot grow old? Because there is only One Mind in the universe and we use It. That Mind is God, that Mind is our mind *now*. How could we wear It out or use It up or exhaust Its possibilities? But we can become so confined in our thinking that It does not reflect or flow through us with clarity. There is no physiological or psychological reason, from the viewpoint of God, that anything could ever be used up or exhausted because nothing is static—everything is a continual flow of Life. When we refuse the flow at whatsoever age we may be, we begin to feel "dead on our feet," as the saying goes. This does not mean that God has changed or denied us any degree of life, but that we have blocked ourselves from our Source.

What would happen if we were free from all fear, or doubt, or the unhappiness and morbidity of our retrospections of the past and the unwholesome anticipation of what we think the future holds in store; from sandwiching the day in which we live between two impossible negations? Somewhere along the line we, who are born to be free, must think our way through until we are no longer afraid of the universe in which we live, until a conviction has dawned in our consciousness that will bring us a solidarity and an integrity which cannot be shaken.

What proof have we outside our desire, our intuition—which would be enough for me—of immortality? In psychological laboratories they have demonstrated that we can experience many of the activities of the organs of sense without using the organs. We can see without the eyes, hear without the ears, speak without the tongue, communicate, travel without the ordinary methods; there is something in us that can function without the body and without the brain. It is not that we do not need brains, but the brains do not think—they are but the instrumentalities of That which is above them and superior to them. This is why Jesus said: "Before Abraham was, I am . . . Destroy this temple, and in three days I will raise it up."

Many who have begun to investigate such facts to dis prove them have come to devote all their time to proving them. There is no question but that they have scientifically disclosed beyond the possibility of chance the ongoingness of the soul. This is why Jesus said to the thief on the cross beside him: "To day shalt thou be with me in paradise." Now if it is true that there is That within us which transcends the use of the physical senses, could it not mean that we are immortal now? The materialistic concept of life has been completely annihilated.

This is the great truth of our being: We are forever individualizing the Spirit, the Spirit is forever unifying with Its own individualization; which means we live in God and God is what we are. Why, then, if these things are true, should we not enter into the spirit of our immortality right now? Carl Jung, whom I consider one of the greatest psychologists, has said that he never knew a case of permanent healing without a restoration of faith, he never knew a person who could be happy the latter part of his life unless he believed in immortality. Why? Because he has nothing to look forward to. It is only in the attention we give to the present, and the certainty we have of its expansion into what we call the future, and the continuity of ongoing, that we would have any joy at all.

Why, then, do we need to feel we must wait to become immortal when it is something we may see and feel and know and understand right now? Growing old is refusing to grow every day, a waiting until that final moment when we step into the larger life. We should be children playing on the shores of time. We miss our friends, we long for the touch of a vanished hand, or the sound of a voice that is stilled. We would not have it otherwise. But there is no hopelessness; there has been but a loosing and liberating from what is no longer needed.

But suppose, right now, we become resurrected and, one by one, remove out of the tomb of memory the fears and morbidities and uncertainties, the hates and jealousies and animosities—everything that is vindictive—and resurrect only that which can bring joy into life. Why is it that down the avenues of evolution, in the begetting of all the great religious systems, which are so good otherwise, they had to drag the corpse and morbidity of sin and punishment and chagrin up the pathway to eternal God and blot out the light of heaven with a shadow of fear?

We should resurrect ourselves, even as Jesus did, to the joy and simplicity and spontaneity of Life. God is no task-master. The eternal Law of Love cannot hurt. That which is Light will never produce darkness. Heaven will never descend into a hell, and a hymn of hate will not stimulate the mind to the harmonies of Life. For our resurrection today must leave the corpses of our dead yesterdays in the tomb of their own obscurity. We must live more abundantly in the God of heaven and earth—awake to God within us this day. Jesus has left us the hope which must be realized. You and I must and shall come out of our tomb of ignorance and disbelief. How glorious shall be the dawn!

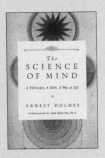

A Treasury of Inspiration and Guidance

A New Design for Living

978-1-58542-814-4

Love and Law

978-1-58542-302-6

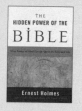

The Hidden Power of the Bible

978-1-58542-511-2

The Essential Ernest Holmes

978-1-58542-181-7

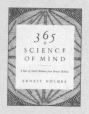

365 Science of Mind

978-1-58542-609-6

Prayer

978-1-58542-605-8

Simple Guides for Ideas in Action

Coming Soon

Questions and Answers on the Science of Mind

Think Your Troubles Away

It's Up to You

Mind Remakes Your World

TARCHER
PENGUIN

For more information:
www.penguin.com
www.tarcherbooks.com
www.scienceofmind.com